THE PLACES THAT BUILT ME

BUILT ME

A Life Made in Hard Places

A MEMOIR BY MICHAEL REED

The Places That Built Me

Copyright© 2025 Michael Reed

Contents

Chapter 1
The Boy in the Corner

The Room Where It Began

My name is Michael Reed, and I was born small in a world that never felt small.

It was in winter 1959 when my first cries reverberated in a small one room bed-sit that could barely accommodate my mom (Elsie) and my dad (Arthur). There were broken plaster, and jangling windows, which shook as trains crashed by. One stove was all we had to keep warm, and it left the flavour of burnt coal in us.

I remember the sound of trains more than their visuals. Their hum was the beat of our home, an inexorable reminder that life outside never stopped, even when ours did.

My father was a railwayman, and he left before sunrise and came back after sunset, with the smell of iron dust and fatigue. He was not much of a talker, not because he was indifferent, but because life had already had its say. He had hard hands and heavy eyes. I thought of whether he could hear the whistle when he went home or whether he had learned to seal it up.

Elsie, my mother, had not much to say. She was a dinner lady in the local school, so she fed those children who were more privileged but oblivious. She hummed as she cooked, and I was so sure that she was talking to herself one time. The fragrance of cabbage, soap, and warm bread was her odour, like a sweet ghost that hanged. She had yearned after such little things as clean tablecloths, working clocks, a family who laughed more than fought.

It was a very small bedsit in which my father almost bumped into the walls as he approached. The roof had a depression, and the rain was murmuring at a hole, filling a rustic old tin pot by the window. Nevertheless, the room was very narrow and contained all my knowledge: hunger, heat, hope, and noises.

As a child, I didn't understand the word poor. To me, life just was. Walls were intimate as that is the manner of building houses. People talked like neighbours shouted. Night was very long since trains never stopped.

As soon as my father came back, the air changed. He would sit at the little table, with a broken mug of tea in his hand, looking at nothing. I would stand and stare, watching my mother, and be on the alert of his temper. I came to know how to read their silence: a profound silence implied no ask, whereas a gentle silence implied he could listen.

Sometimes, I would wake up late at night and heard some whispered worries about rent, bills and broken shoes. Yes, we will, said Elsie to me, we will. We always do." Arthur grunted half in hope and half submission.

There was a metal-framed bed that had a thin mattress which squeaked every time anyone would turn. I shared my bed between my parents until I was big enough to be shoved to the periphery. During cold nights, Elsie's hand used to touch mine, and it rubs gently to make me feel warmer. The softness of that stroke remains the tenderest that I have.

There was a smell of coal smoke and tea leaves in the mornings. Arthur went off with his lunch-basket, Elsie with her apron under her coat. I saw them at the window, and I had a finger to a cold glass hoping that they would not turn back up the lane to the station. The room was again quiet, excepting the ticking clock and the trains in the distance.

Words could not change me as much as silence did. I learned to listen in that silence, to the humming of the stove, kettle-sigh, creaking floor boards. They would be lessons in themselves. The world speaks in low tones to people who have grown up in small areas.

Elsie very frequently carried home what she had brought to school: a slice of pudding, a half-loaf of bread, and we would divide it like a feast. She would smile, and tell me, "Oh, see, Michael, there is always enough, so long as you are grateful to it." I did not yet understand that it was hunger and faith that made her grateful.

Arthur laughed, seldom and sincerely. It shocked me--a harsh laugh, as rocks in a tub--but it filled up the room. These short experiences made me realize that inside even the most difficult men there is a spot of sunlight.

Time did not progress normally in that little room. The days passed, train, work, sleep, repeat, till the only measure of a new day was the quantity of soot adhering to the boots of Arthur.

Motion was a life form to my parents, a puzzle to me, how come the outside world was in so much hurry and we were sitting still.

After a long time, I started observing life off the tracks. I would tap the wall with my ear at night and daydream about the destinations of the trains- destinations of light, laughter and people who do not stress about pennies. I never knew their names, but I thought they were there. That belief seeded hope in me.

In retrospect I find our one room bedsit was not just a home it was a teacher. It was a demonstration of how to live with no thinking small, how to listen, how to wait. The trains were a lesson of being patient, my parents a lesson of being enduring. I came to know that life does not begin with much, it begins cramped, bent up the wall, lurking till someone courageous takes a step.

The First School Bell

When I was four I found my world extended outside our bedsit.

The first morning of school my mother, Elsie, twisted my hair with her fingers and buttoned my coat all the way up. She got down to my level and told me, "Be brave, Michael. Listen to your teacher." I nodded--as though valor were a sort of button.

The walk to the school seemed to be long. The road was damp and glittering; our feet produced little noise by treading on the rocks. On the other side of the gates, other children were holding on to the hands of their mothers. Some cried. Some ran in circles. I waited, and observed the doors opening. A bell sounded--sweet and solemn--as of the beginning of something significant.

Everything indoors smelt of polish and chalk. The bright posters were filmed on the walls: letters, numbers and smiling animals which appeared to be aware of secrets. We were seated in a little classroom furnished with small desks that had lids and a blackboard at the back of the desk of the teacher. She had a flower-shaped pin and a cardigan on her. "Good morning," she said. "I'm your teacher." Her smile was frozen, as in a picture.

We were taught how to put up coats. We learned where to sit. We were taught to put hands and leave feet at rest. I made an attempt, I felt like I must be good. I had a desire to be a type of boy who would make my mother proud. In cases where the teacher had created a large A on the board, white on black, the other children followed suit. They resembled a unison scratching of pencils. I sank my pencil, and the line was trembling. My A was as broken as a ladder.

We moved to B and C. My letters fell over like fatigued men. When the teacher paused to look, she tapped desks between the rows using a ruler. She paused at mine. No, no, said she, not unkindly, but not soft either. She switched my paper and put her hand on the paper to show the direction of the pencil. The letter was also well-written under her hand, rather than mine. As she went away the shapes were scattered asunder.

Reading time came after milk. There were simple words in the book: cat, mat, sat. The other children used turns and the sounds fell out of their mouth as though they were born knowing how. When I came to it the letters rose and swam. I realized that they were meant to arrive in sequence, yet they would not. I attempted to guess what the picture was. The instructor corrected and instructed me to check the letters. I stared further; they stared at me like they were strangers.

The line would not stay still. The letters fell and folded, now this side, now that, round about. My mouth went dry. I said nothing.

"It's simple," she said. "Everyone else can do it."

Heat climbed up my neck. I got a sound--any sound--and relieved myself. It wasn't the right one. A few children giggled. The teacher pulled a breath in her nose and repeated the word vicariously. "Again," she said. The giggling had diminished to a little wave.

When it was time to play at school I did not run. I walked to the end of the playground and had pressed my palms on the coarse brick. I heard the other children scream, run after and laugh. One of the little boys wearing a red scarf wanted to play. I said perhaps some other time, and he shrugged and went. One by one by one I took the letters out on the wall with my finger: A, B, C. They were good on brick, and useless on paper.

The days went like that. As we sat at our desks we practiced letters, mine being in the habit of sitting with his back turned. In the reading circle, it changed when it was my turn. I was taught to count the spaces till I came to me, and then cough or drop my pencil or shake my head like I had a sore throat. Sometimes it worked. Sometimes it didn't.

One afternoon the teacher pinned the sheets of our handwriting. Other children had the neat rows. Mine was not on the wall. She held it in her hand and called me up. "Michael," she said, "look at this. This is messy. This is... not trying." She neither screamed nor spoke, but her mouth was drawn up. The class looked at me. Their eyes were little lamps; I could feel them burning.

I would have liked to say to her that I was trying. I would have said that my mind was compartmented like a drawer that all the things were moved aside at the back when I opened it. But I could not describe how it was. I had no idea even that there were words. And when you lack the right words, silence comes in and fills your spaces.

I had never heard the word dunce, the first time it was uttered was through the lips of a teacher and it sounded like a drop of ice. She uttered it, but not too faintly that I could hear. "Don't be a dunce." Instead, it suspended in the air above my desk and then penetrated me. The laugh that ensued was not loud, merely a little quail, the kind of laugh that causes one to be shrunken even after it is gone. The corner came later. Be there, she told and pointed towards the back of the room. "Face the wall."

The color had been cold and pale. My legs desired to shake, and the wall was the only one standing still, so I lay my cheek against it. The lesson went on in my absence--reading, copying, whispering. I saw the dark hand of the clock go crawling along the wall. If I cried, it would be worse. So, I didn't. I choked back the tears and allowed them to rest somewhere.

I was told that I could not learn, and I believed them a long time. At home, I told no one. Mom inquired about my school performance, and I replied that everything was fine. She cleaned my face with a wet cloth and had to set the table. My father gazed at his tea, like it had the answer and he could not locate it. I maintained a stare on the spoons and the little ray of light under the lamp.

The following day, the teacher told me to repeat the reading. I would have been so like to be on the side, I drew a breath and ventured. The letters melted away, and the sounds were rubbing against each other, and then there was the laughter, at first soft, and then more lusty. The ruler of the board was used by the teacher. "Quiet," she said. She spelled the word out in big letters and uttered it gradually. As I said it the second time, she did not compliment me, but she nodded. Only children who were able to do it the first time were praised, I learnt.

Another teacher occasionally came to our classroom. She had glasses that gave her eyes a kind appearance. Once she came knelling beside my desk asking me to read one word. "Take your time," she said. I did and it was still incorrect. She gave me a pat on the shoulder and said that there was nothing to worry about. There was a moment of lightening of the room. That night I fancied that letters in a line were like little soldiers, that did what they was told to do. In the morning they were rebels once more.

The corner changed me. At first, it was humiliation. Later it turned into something different. I listened with my face to the wall. I also got to know the rhythm of the room, the scratching of good pencils, the sound of two pages turning in unison, the up and down of the voice of the teacher when she was happy or weary. I used the soft clicks of the clock. By the coolness of the light on the plaster I could tell when the sun went behind a cloud. No one expected anything of me, so I saw everything.

I began to draw in my mind. Unless letters would, pictures would. I thought of the trains, how they rattled before they came, and sketched their figures in my mind. I sketched the hands of my mother, the feet of my father, the crack in the ceiling over our bed. I came to those pictures when I was sent to the corner. They belonged to me, and they never laughed.

One day the teacher told us that we were to read out of the Bible. She referred to it as a good book to know how to sound out words. We were in a queue and alternated. As the book fell on me the text knotted up. I looked so long at the page that the edges became blurred. Someone snickered. The teacher reclaimed the book and said, Sit down. I did, my ears burning. The red scarfed boy read my line instead. He got a gold star.

My mother actually held my face in her hands that evening, and said to me, you are a good boy, Michael. Do not be made small by any person. Nodded, but I was no larger than a thumb. I would have told her that it was not my choice to be small, but it was the choice of letters that ran. Yet mothers have enough weight. I kept that one for myself.

Weeks turned into months, and I got to know how to survive school. I sat somewhere that I could not be easily seen by the teacher. I volunteered to wipe brushes or distribute books-- anything that would make me move. I knew which children would smile and which children preferred whispering. I was taught to breathe slowly when the name was called, as a swimmer does who is holding air.

What I did not know were those things that the wall charts promised: how the alphabet lines went so sweetly, how the numbers went in a row and never hit each other. These would follow, in another form, another way, and by other doors. So far on, school was where the world wanted one type of clever and I was another type.

It softened something in me when, years later, I came to know the name of what had snagged my letters. But there was no name then--there was only the corner and the laugh and the taste of tears in your mouth till they became salty.

I can forgive the children. They were just being children-- exploring and locating themselves in the pack. And even the teachers were doing with what they knew. The system was fond of lines and boxes and I could not fit into either. I never used to realize that not fitting did not mean failing.

As I shut my eyes now, I can still feel the cold cheek of the wall against my cheek and feel the soft use of the clock over it. I can even smell the dust of chalk and polish on the floor. And I may yet see the front of the room door which shines with outside light, which waits on the day when I might learn to study differently--with wind in it and with engines and with wide openness to the life which needed not perfect letters to initiate it.

The Corner Prison

By the age of six I owned the corner. It was waiting to me each morning as definitely as the sound of the bell or the chalk dust in the air. I was sent there sometimes because I read too slowly, sometimes because I wrote letters backwards and sometimes because I was never told why. The teacher would stand there and point with her ruler. And make them all witness, when you fail to attempt. And so, I stood.

Initially I believed it was because I was being punished because of being lazy as they informed me. But I wasn't lazy. I was trying--trying harder than anybody could know. The more

I tried, the worse it appeared to be. The wall was my audience, so primitive and cracked was its paint, that nothing there was laughing or sighing when I failed.

Days blurred into weeks. My classmates did not even pay attention to the fact that I went to the corner; it was a manner of things. When the teacher would say, Eyes forward, I would vanish out of their world, squashed into mine. I started to describe it as my cell prison, small place where time does not pass and words cannot reach me.

I can recall the coldness that resided there. The wall was never warm, not even in summer. I would lean my cheek against it and hear. I could hear the humming of voices in the background, the scratching of seats, and the monotonous tapping of pencils. In some cases, the voice of the teacher could be heard, high and fatigued. Other occasions she did not even hear me at all because I had become the paint.

I attempted to pass the time at first by counting, counting seconds, counting cracks, counting breaths. Then I started talking to the wall, not speaking. Only one person did not interrupt or correct me: it was the only listener. I explained to it that I had dreams of having a motorbike and that one day I would be riding that far that no one could make me stand on the ground again. I explained to it about the smile on my mother and the silence of my father. I was telling it what I could never say.

I thought soon that the wall understood me better than others. It realized how much I was afraid of the ruler and how scared I was of the word read and how small was my pride whenever I could spell my own name correctly. It did not criticise when I fell, or spoke when I wept. It was there, all right, steady, solid, safe.

I would tell it when no one was looking that, they said I could not learn, but perhaps I could hear. And that's what I did. I heard him standing in that corner. I got to know the beat of the classroom, and the ups and downs of laughter, and the clatter of pencils scurrying, and the chasis when they were lost. When the teacher was fatigued, when the students were active, and when it had begun raining behind the glass before anybody had heard, I was able to tell.

Isolation increased my perception. As they were learning words and sums, I was learning people. I was able to read faces and not able to read books. I had read the gentleness of a mouth, the bitterness of eyes. I discovered that pity is as hurtful as teasing, as silence is also a weapon and a shield.

One afternoon had left itself in my memory. The headmaster visited. He walked into our room in big shoes and a gleaming smile. The teacher pulled himself down, the pupils sat up, and I stood--already in my corner. What the hell is that boy doing there, he asked. She smiled politely. "That's Michael Reed, sir. He's a bit slow. I hold him there to remind the rest what they do when they fail to put into practice." He nodded approvingly. "Every class needs an example." The term example struck like a curse in my head. I would no longer be a boy, I would be a warning, a signpost of failure that lived.

On the evening when I was coming home, I attempted to scratch the word out of me. I kicked my feet on the dirt, wiped my hands on the fence, wishing it would remain there, but it accompanied me all the way home. No amount of voice on the part of my mother could cleanse it. You are a good boy, Michael, you see, drying my hands with my apron. "Just keep trying." I would have liked to inform her that it did not matter anymore, the wall had already taken me.

But something strange had just commenced growing in that silence--a stubborn spark. When the teacher said, you will never learn, it was a little voice in me and it said, watch me. It wasn't loud yet. It wasn't strong. But it was there. The wall had taught me to listen and I was now starting to listen to myself.

I began to see little success. I would be able to write my name without turning the letters. I was able to check time with the classroom clock. I might be standing my ground and be proud that I was not crying. Everything was a revolt, something that no one could notice other than myself.

Once, when the other children looked at me, I looked at them and smiled, but not to seek friendship, but to remind them that I was still there, still a human, still something larger than the example they supposed I was. The corner had made to be my prison, yes, but also my training ground. Each humiliation made me tougher so that I will not break the next time.

Had you entered that classroom, you could have found a boy standing still against the wall with his head bent down and his hands motionless. However, there was another thing occurring in there. Within, a head was to learn how to live. One heart was getting to know how to beat without applause. Some soul was teaching it, that silence might be a virtue.

Then years after, as I went back, I saw that that corner never ruined me, it made me up. It taught me the form of loneliness, however, the sound of resilience. It taught me that no matter how the world can turn its back to you, it never stops being one-on-one.

Thus the wall, which had enclosed me, was my first friend. It was not liberating me through words, but through patience. On its cold surface I was reflected, --not a dunce, not a failure, merely a boy with a lot to make to show them all.

A Hidden World

Where the room seemed claustrophobic, I sought a spot where I did not have to be clever. I discovered it at the outskirts of our village, where the houses became more sparse and the soil became wild. Beyond a crooked gate and a narrow path was a bit of woods that people in the vicinity hardly noticed. It was a totally new country to me.

The initial occasion I went out alone was when it was light and the air had a fragrance of rain. The trees were silent individuals, and their branches swept against one another in a whispering air. My footwear was wet in the loose soil and something within me unscrewed. No letters. No ruler tapping a desk. Practicing their own languages, and not corrected.

The woods restored my size to me, in case the classroom had reduced me. Beyond the trees the land was cleared into the clay-pits of ponds--vast, silent basins abandoned by labor that had long since lost its object. Dragonflies fluttered over them as gleaming knives, and the air was cool and swept the schoolroom out of me.

I wasn't always alone. Sometimes, my classmate Tommy ran with me -two doors down, quick legs, laugh that shook the trees. He was the good kind that earned stickers at school, but none of that here. He would beat his own shadow and time was measured by his ability to hold his breath.

You can never get to the opposite bank, I bet you can't, he would say and splash down, leaving a line of bubbles. I trailed behind--not to win, but to have the water close over my head and the world grow soft. The whole process came down to the monotony of the arms and legs under the surface.

Our mate, Nina occasionally greeted us at the gate, little and trim with a plait and a pocket always containing a sweet. She was not as fast as Tommy but she could see what other people overlooked. She would sit down on a log with her knees together and watch us skipstones. When I handled three skips she clapped and said, for you, and gave me a mint. It was sweet and warm like sugar and love, both of which are worth keeping until they are melted.

School was not discussed much. There were other subjects in the woods, the prints of foxes, and all the arguments whether the big pond was endless. Let me drop a stone here, Tommy said, and it will come out in China. Nina rolled her eyes. Stones do not move, said she, and gave me a half toffee. She was a mixture of nonsense and sweetness.

Nature made me her most excellent instructor. It taught by means of generating equilibrium and repercussion: a sloppy log had to be handled; brambles corrected lust; a startled bird made it known that sometimes the only way to get out was up. I sat down, was scratched, got wet and learned. Failure out here was only drill in another coat.

And the earth smelt like fresh coins and pulverized leaves after rain. Nina came carrying three barley sugars in wrapper twisty papers. "You get two," she said. "Tommy stole mine last time." He smiled and made off with one. We were laughing like children when the world was big and time had lost count.

The day I was practicing non-action. Then I stood at the water till my reflection ceased shivering--thin, with his hair standing up, with his eyes being too hopeful. I attempted to view myself in the manner in which the pond did, free of grades or titles. Nothing but a boy with scratches on his knees and water on his shoes. The pond did not answer, it kept me down till a wave swept me off.

Occasionally I lay in the clearing, palms to the ground, and the earth was gripping me. The trees were talking in a raving, the restless chatter in a sneezing, the heavy silence of noon, all mumbled in the wind. As the sun was setting the light became gold and the shadows long enough to walk in.

Tommy vowed that there was some secret door in the woods--a hollow between two beeches where a fox trail thru the bracken chopped. Without saying a word, he walked away and indeed found himself in a better place. The attempt was frequent, grave and quiet, at all events on the same clearing. I never explained to him what I thought: that it was in trees that the door was—it was in us. You pass when you have confidence in your feet than in the fear.

During the most unpleasant school-days--the ruler shrewd, the laugh cruel--Nina used to stay behind the gate at the end of the school day. "Walk?" she'd ask. She didn't pry. We would go out in their clearing where she would tell me small stories: kittens behind the shed, a boy that was stuck half-way up the gym rope, an ice-cream man with a secret notebook of customers. Her narrations were fleets of hard to soft.

16

"Do you ever get in trouble?" I asked.

"Sometimes," she said. "For reading at the table."

"That's trouble?"

Mum says books are fine, but potatos will not peel.

We giggled, and I wondered how certain types of trouble were light to other types of trouble.

I did not tell her of the word dunce. The woods knew it for me. It stained into the bark and dissolved. The school corner had an effect of tightening my chest, the woods had a widening effect. That was the way I understood where the real learning location was.

I knew how to run, not to run over, to stop short. Balance-to walk a fallen tree, hands in the air, head straight. Attention-- to listen to the difference between the hop of a rabbit and the step of a person. Nor did it get stickers, but it all made me strong.

After we made a raft out of scrapwood. The knots of Tommy were like fists, and mine like scared snakes. Nina said she'd be crew only. We hauled it to the nearest pond; and it breathed a giant sigh, and stood under water. We laughed at it so hard we had forgotten to draw it out. "A noble ship," Tommy declared. "Lost at sea," Nina said. I recalled that episode afterwards--three children in the verge of failure, and no one taking them to the corner.

As the light dimmed down we walked home together. Nina shared her final sweet outside the gate, Tommy had just to run faster to break his record. I slowed down. I found the transition between wild and street, the change between moss and coal smoke, between the singing of birds, and the sound of trains, to be pleasant.

At home, Mum enquired, where have you been, love?

"Out," I said.

"Good out or muddy out?"

"Muddy out."

She grinned and took a towel. Dirt never earned scolding. This dirt was a sign that I had not been in the corner. Dad was already there sometimes with boots off and eyes away. He would look at my scratched knees and not say anything. We had dissimilar maps his of rails and my of paths.

My days at the ponds were followed by the best of my sleep. The trains beyond were no longer reminders, they were lines, lines that were drawn across the world. I shut my eyes, and touched the bark with my hands, cool water with my flesh, the sugar-sweet present of a mint.

I later on realized: school made me know how small I could be but wood made me know how big I was already. The ponds showed a boy not broken, but just made in other ways. The wind said keep going. The trees said stand steady. The path said move. And I did.

Eleven and Earning

Two things I had known by eleven, the first that school would leave me without any of my pride, the second that money could restore a slice of the same.

The idea that would not get out of my mind began when I had seen my father on his counting, at the table, in a straight line, and sliding one coin into his pockets, as though he were apologizing to him. The burden of poverty strained me despite me not being aware of our debts. I had a glimpse of their faces worn out shoes, snorting kettle, my mother banging bacon like one slice will nourish two.

One afternoon I saw, in the shop-window: Paper boy wanted. Morning round. The letters were mute, monotonous, since they talked of a promise. I entered the house and cleared my throat. "I can do it," I told the clerk. He looked up at me, thin, grave, older than I was at all bad ways, and, he said, you will have to be up before light. I nodded; I was already rising early before day because anxiety roused early.

It was so cold in the morning I thought it would break. The pile of newspapers was higher than my stomach and tied up in twine, which burnt my fingers pulling it off. I carried the canvas bag on my shoulder and walked out. The streets were still. Milk bottles were like dozy soldiers standing on doorsteps. Once a dog cawed and recalled the time of day and ceased.

In no time I was familiar with the round: what letterboxes sting, what gates wail, what old fellow fakes sleep but listens like a bell to the heavy beat of paper. I was making little ghosts of my breath; the strap pricked my shoulder, but I felt something warm under the cold, the correctness of travelling in a world which did not populate me.

By week end the shopkeeper gave me a pile of small coins. I did not count them, at first, I simply held them, keeping the palms closed, and feeling the weight. It was the first that I had ever possessed, neither on loan, or on the condition of a pledge, mine. I got home more slowly than normal as though the coins were going to know how to fly in case I went fast. My mother looked at my hands, and then at my face, and kissed my hair without saying anything, in the doorway. This was her manner of telling she was proud.

When I had time to make it to the second round, I did it, including getting up earlier than the other time to get another shipment before the weather switched. Saturdays I was at the greengrocer--piling apples with the shiny ones on my outside, and sweeping up the floor when the mud had left a pattern of the shoes of every one. It was the man of there that referred to me as a quiet lad and gave me a bruised pear at noon. "It tastes the same," he said. It did.

The coins came with pride and loneliness. When other boys were sleep or changing football cards, I knew the outline of the village at daybreak--who closed their curtains, those who left bicycles uncovered, those who listened to the radio so faintly it was a secret. Saturdays I had found children of my own age quarrelling over candies and I had been counting the change with numb fingers. I envied them, sometimes--the play they had taken so naturally, the by-word laugh. Then I put my hand in the pocket I was earning and recalled what I was making.

I did not spend the money initially. I preserved it in a jam jar. The glass smelled slightly of strawberries when you put your nose to it; I made myself not to. I wanted the coins to stink of metal and hard work. I took the jar out at night and tilted it and the coins slid and making a noise. There was nothing like that sound to put a child to sleep. It could be that tomorrow would be more than today.

The work strengthened me in the aspects that no one graded. My hands toughened. My feet learned distance. My head knew streets, time, and how to keep time when you opened the door on time. I found out that the world could make sense in other ways that did not need letters to act.

On a Sunday once, I was meeting Tommy and Nina by the gate.

"Come to the pond," Tommy, said and was already running.

"Can't," I said. "Round morning, shop after."

He made a face. "All day?"

"We can go later, Nina," said the softer. I shook my head and at one time I felt older than both of them, not in an arrogant manner, but in a way that was hurtful and a little bit. "

Another day," I promised.

Everybody was aware that promises are the most convenient things to spend.

As soon as the jar became heavy enough to bend the shelf I began to plan. I did not use fancy words such as goal and investment. I had an image, two rims, a small seat, a painted tank. I had seen one before, the older boys riding it up and down the lane into the woods and laughing at the ends of the streamers. When I turned round, they were shadows, though the sound remained--a low, confident roar, which seemed to be a beat of the heart which you could grasp in your hands.

I posed to the shopkeeper whether he knew anybody who would be selling a small motorbike. He questioned and said, you bound to the clouds? Just the fields, I replied. He smiled as he knew the difference.

The weeks stacked. The jar filled. My back had made the price of early mornings, and my breast had made the gift of them. I was weary, all right, though it was a good weary like the one that follows the choice of your own pain. My hands shook once I had got the coins spilled over on the table and counted them up to a purpose. My dad sat on his chair with no readable eyes. "What's that for?" he asked.

"A machine," I said.

Once he nodded but slowly and returned to his tea. That was his blessing.

I had had a bad night, the sort a man has just before the object of his desire has an opportunity to happen. I was riding already, in my dreams: the village is blur behind, the fields a green sea, and my name called by no one, because the wind had taken it. I got up earlier than the alarm and was lying in the gray light, listening to the trains. And this was the first time that their sound did not seem to me to be life passing by--it was a roll of the drum.

I had coins in brown paper in my pockets, and I could not even make my mouth smile or pray. Between the stalls and the grease and the men who knew a life story about every bolt, I came upon what I wanted. But that is another story.

The Freedom Machine

She was not good-looking in any sense: she had peeling paint, a dented tank, a sew-up seat. But when the seller began her and that BSA Dandy cleared its throat until it was running, there was something in my chest like a door that I had been kicking against my entire life.

The noise was not loud, but constant and persistent - a beat you could feel in your flesh. The air smoked of petrol, and its sting was sharp enough to open my eyes and clear my head. I went round the bike twice, feigning to inspect it, when in fact what I was doing was memorizing: the gloss of the chrome, the shape of the clutch cable, the little clock that appeared willing to keep my time.

A hundred and fifty, said the man. She's honest. I pushed a pack of coins in every direction. My breath was between boy and almost-man. It was heavier than it appeared, as he gave me the key, small and cold. Being independent is like that - too light to feel until you hold it.

The first kick failed. The second sputtered. The third roared. The scramble very much up my leg to my ribs. The bench was smaller than I thought but it belonged to me. The handlebars suit me like chance suits fortune. I slipped the clutch and crept on--slowly, then faster and fences and sky becoming one long blinding streak.

I was paddled on by the wind and it told the truth: the world could not pass by me, but past me. The street sang under narrow tires, and I got to know in a breath what the schoolroom never taught me, that the wheel of my story was in my own hands.

In the beginning I remained in lanes in the hedge tunnels. The odour of petrol was mixed with the damp grass. Birds came out in front as commas in an incomplete sentence. My hands were fluent in a language that my head was not allowed to know.

I drove her towards the fields. Air burnt, and cured simultaneously. I laughed at it, and quickly, unbelieving. They had termed me slow, uninstructable, corner-fitting. But this time, as the road was unfolding and the engine responding to me, I felt invulnerable.

The initial error occurred at the clay-pit circuit. Rocks rolled; the hind-wheel slide. A moment I was on my side, the world tilted. School whispered a voice, See you can't. I relaxed, with head forward, as woods had taught. The tire was hooked, the line drawn. I patted the tank. "Sorry," I said. The bike forgave me. Machines, as trees, demand nothing but attention.

Tommy, looking out of his gate, ran in the road with his arms open. "No way!" as though I had come out of the future, he shouted. He tottered off next to me, with flapping shoes.

"Can I—?"

"Later," I said, not brutally, only keeping watch over what had cost me all my money saved. He grinned. "You look like you can fly."

For once, I believed it.

Nina stood there on the hedge, timidly smiling, sweet in hand. She touched the seat, reverently with two fingers. "Is it safe?" I asked. "Safer than school," I replied. She laughed, because it was not a joke.

I got acquainted with the machine as I familiarized myself with woods, by texture. Where the clutch catches. How the brakes give warning of a bite. The tone change of the engine when you push too hard or even more than that. I rode round until my wrists ached and stalling no longer stinged.

On the other side of the ponds was a long ribbon of dirt. I opened the throttle. I could ride on the roar that was like a heartbeat. The hedges blurred behind me. The world became one straight, shiny line and falling ceased to be in the formula. The air was welcoming to me.

As evening fell to gold I drove home, the engine clacking down. Going through the school, I caught sight of the windows small, boring, harmless at this moment. I almost saw the boy that had stood up there with his cheek to the wall. I didn't hate him. I would have said to him: wait; here the road is coming.

Mum was standing in the doorway back home, with her hand to her mouth. Michael, she said, three meanings at a time. Dad went out, circled the bike, and nodded his head. "Mind the brakes," he said. "They're liars." It was the first sentence he had ever given me in weeks. I stored it up; advice is also a type of fuel.

No matter how much I rubbed my hands that night, they had a petrol smell. I didn't mind. I was in bed and the phantom vibration in my bones had stopped, the hum had settled. We were in harmony with the trains outside which were singing their iron song. Movement now belonged to me.

School didn't change. The words continued to revolve, the teachers continued to sigh. However, I was harboring a secret a machine that could ferry me past all the sneers. They had ladders in their world; I had roads.

On Sundays I rode to the ponds, and parked under the hanging beech. Tommy lamented to have a turn; I allowed him to take his seat with the engine off. Nina slipped something sweet under the seat, and hoped this would bring luck, luck being fuel. We discussed wind and balance, grade and corners were forgotten.

I named the bike something that I did not utter. Certain names are retained by me. I said so when I kicked her to life and she replied in a hissing.

A skinny boy on a little machine might have looked like a normal one even far away. But even in the smile I could not repress, there was something still greater. Still there was a gear of freedom, and I had discovered it.

The road did not inquire of whether I was able to read or not; it inquired whether I was able to listen, balance, and breathe. I could.

Mornings cold and dark that winter, but I still rose earlier than light. I still did my rounds. The road between doorsteps was now mine. There was a boy somewhere in a corner behind a window in a classroom learning to be small. I passed by him, not away, but by. Due to the fact that I would require both boys in what was to follow; the one who survived and the one that fled.

The Family Table

Evenings at home were smaller by the time the bike had learned my hands, as though the walls had moved in my absence. The kitchen was filled with the smell of soap, and onions and the lean, gallant roast my mother could make out of almost nothing. Below it was another smell: the silence of anxiety. Anxiety is like the pot that has been boiled down.

Mum — Elsie Reed — was setting out dishes just as she always did, when her gaze kept snatching at the window where night was edging so close to the glass, beyond which lay my BSA Dandy in the lane. My father, --Arthur, --was sitting just out of the table, without his boots, his socks mended, his shoulders stooped down as though they were still dangling. He cut the meat into good clean and even slices, the knife glittering, falling in the same tired fashion as it had fallen with all the work in his life.

"Wash your hands, love," Mum said. I did, but not even a lot of soap could take away the smell of petrol which had penetrated my skin. I sat, minding not to tell how I had ridden down the lane, nor how the wind had whistled through my sleeves. The bicycle was still throbbing in my chest like a secret beat that shook my spoon.

Arthur lifted his cup. Be careful of the brakes, said he, as I have just said. I test them on straight, I answered. "Ease, then squeeze." He nodded once. "Good." The fibre between us unraveled, in its turn.

Mum glared at us, as a person takes care of a small flame. How is your round, Michael? Fine. Dog of Mrs. Doyle loose? Chained today.

She gave me a slice of bread, toasted it, and buttered it, and then cut it very neatly up to the edges so I would not have any bite that was dry. She could make not-enough seem to be plenty. We ate at the forks and exhales. The radio mumbled softly. There went a train passing out of doors, the old heartbeat of the house. It no longer matched mine. The piston was followed by my pulse.

Don't ride after dark, Mum said lightly, voice wrapped round fear. It is not dusk dark, I said, not so that I am. Arthur cleared his throat. "Dusk hides potholes." He did not look at me; he simply got butter on the sides of his bread.

What I wanted to say to them was that it was not rebellion, it was discipline, patience, focus. But there are certain facts that cannot be translated. Mum brought the dishes, piled them up, hands traced with the narrative of her day: heat, cold, mute expectation. You will grow out of it, sink, she said. Boys do, I told myself, meaning it myself.

When dinner was over Arthur went to the wireless and heard people talking about the weather, wages, and matches. He didn't ask about the road. He had his rails; I had mine. We had two maps closely together, and never crossed.

Mum went wafting up and down between us, the dishcloth on her shoulder like a white flag. She smiled to me as though she said be nice, and to him as though she said be long-suffering. I wanted to be both. I also wanted to ride.

"I'll just—" I began.

She said masculinely, but gently, Michael. "Put your scarf on. The damp gets in your chest."

"Yes, Mum." I put the wool around without protest, only impatiently. At the door, I heard the image of Arthur in the dark mirror. His eyes, but not head, elevated. "Back before full dark," he said. Something tender within it like a bruise not to press. "I will," I promised.

The evening had the bluest air of all outside. And the bike was waiting, waiting, machines waiting. I flicked the key, kicked and the noise came up the lane like air back into lungs. The cutlery in the kitchen shook in the vibration. Mum would be wiping dishes; Arthur would be listening uncertainly proud and scared.

I turned to the head of the street and took a peep behind. The house was like a warm square, with a glow. I experienced the attraction of both worlds, the cautious table, the anxious hands, the silent father, a little. Then I relaxed the clutch and left the lane to me. The initial revolt of my life was not vocal. It was movement, a boy on a small machine, preference of motion to permission.

Sundays of Normal

When Sundays started to come out of shape at thirteen. They had been reliable and had been predictable once, bells in church, roast in the oven, shirts on the line, neighbours waving. The day moved like a hymn. Two had lunch, four had a listen on the radio, warm laundry off the line, and folded.

Now there were blank places in the list where I was lost. Mum continued to roast the roast with her devotion, and turned the pan like a good and a bad side to meat. She even used the old plates, the blue ringed ones. Still she wanted me to take the gravy boat, feigning the dinner hung on it. It was all I did, moved, hauled, nodded, only, my mind ran in the deep tread of an engine that was about to begin moving.

Arthur was precise with his chisels. "...Stretch it," he said to himself, the old rule of years when meat must feed too many. He did not look at me, nor did I look at him. He added another piece on the plate of Mum. She pretended not to see. Such was the sound of apologies in our house--voiceless apologies.

On some Sundays we would walk to my aunt. It was a road that passed allotments and sheds in which the men stood imitating gardening, and exchanging opinion. To Arthur they bowed their caps. He nodded back. The three seconds of respect were the closest he had to joy.

There was a different silence at our own table, though not acute, but only padded, battered at use. Mum talked into it, and tried to stuff it without rupturing it. Did you see the new sign at the shop, Michael, she would ask? Which one? Bus times changed again. Mm. Arthur would add, "Always do." And somehow, that was enough.

I started losing consciousness in tiny harmless manners. Getting bread the long way round. Rambling in the garden at night under the pretext of clothes. Cleaning off dust beneath the seat of the bike where no dust had ever accumulated. Mum saw it — mothers always do.

One Sunday when she was boiling the carrots and roast was resting, she talked without turning. "You'll go far, lad. Just don't forget who you are."

Her words stunned me in the middle of thoughts. "Who am I, then?" I tried to smile it off. She smiled too, tired but kind. You are the one that helps without asking. Who thanks his tea. When to be fast and when to be silent, who knows. She touched my cheek lightly. You mine, she said, not to possess me, but to remind me that possession is not possession but generation.

Arthur cleared his throat, and would have liked to assist in his own awkward fashion. And you are the boy that looks where he is going, he said. Short words, long meaning. His love was in the form of a road sign- spare, convenient, simple to pass over unless you were alert.

In the fall that year fairground posters were beginning to go up- bright and noisy on gray walls. I acted that it didn't matter, but the feeling in my chest was like the engine that was idling. Tommy talked of nothing else. Nina replied that she loved the lights and did not like the noise. I said nothing. I was already feeling the notion of departure resting against my ribs.

Sundays took me now instead of having me. I continued to eat at the table, waved at what Mum was saying about neighbors, who had a baby, who had come to the city, who had taken on a new dog as though it were hope. I saw her looking notice, since love, I had observed, was mostly that, attention.

At dinner time, when the little window was dimed by steam, as a result of the washing-up, I was standing at the back step, in a towel, looking over the garden at the lane leading away. The bicycle was under its tarp like a secret that I would not be able to keep indefinitely. I had heard that home was not a trap It was where the road came in.

On this night, Mum lingered at the table, as the dishes were cleared. She wrapped the cloth on her knee and said, "Promise me something."

I promised her... I said, "You go away you see, when you go, and bring a part of your home with you, now and then. A postcard. A call. Your voice in the kitchen. Anything."

I nodded, throat tight. "I promise."

I had no idea when I would go or whither I would go, but I knew that she was right--I was going far. The promise would follow me everywhere, but it would be the reminder that I will have to be two people at the same time: one who left, and one who stayed.

The Spark before Escape

The fair came as weather. One morning the field at the outskirts of town was deserted; in the afternoon lorries came, and there was the odor of metal and sugar. Men drove posts, lights were knotted like veins over the grass, a Ferris wheel was starting up against the sky like a skeleton learning to walk.

I stood on the lane, feigning indifference, and hands in pockets, and heart a-banging. Posters flapped. Ropes tightened. The rides gave their initial cries--the throat clearing of appliances, and then they started shouting.

By dusk the green was alive. The music was thrust through my chest; smoke whirled; the odour of dough frying mingled with rain which had not yet come. Children were pulling on the hands of their parents like the lights had strained strings that were not visible.

I pulled into the side of the road with the BSA Dandy and walked slowly, allowing the fair to locate my speed. A man shouted, "Win a goldfish!" One of them beat a booth into submission. The sound I heard was a combination of thunder and laughter, of metal and danger. In the light which all were looking a little bolder, a little potential.

One booth a boy tossed toffee apples in air as though he had been making his own fortunes. A man behind him with a pencil behind his ear lit a cigarette and looked on me like a question.

"Work?" he said.

"Maybe," I answered.

"Can you climb?"

"Yes."

Could you not ask too many questions when things are moving?

I smiled. "That's my best thing."

He was indicating the Ferris wheel. We must have hands preceding the lights.

I obeyed, carrying after him what he indicated, teaching by example. All noise and all coordination his crew was on time. And when the initial strand of bulbs burst into light I experienced a gladness which I could not have told--not the gladness of praise, but of purpose.

When the rides were finally opened, I lost myself in the crowd. Nina came in, with a paper bag of hot doughnuts.

"You came," she said.

"Just to look."

She smiled and tore one of them in half. "For courage."

Tommy ran up gasping. "You've got to try the waltzers! They rot you like a top and you lose your name.

"I like my name," I said.

You may as well take it up again, Nina said to herself.

I didn't ride. I watched. The music of the fair and the blackness of the sky combined, and the lights were making ordinary people moving stars.

I also saw a boy in his age walking around the spinning platform in Noah's Ark ride, throwing perfect balance and landing on the painted horses. I would have preferred to be in his position.

"Can I—?" I began.

"Tomorrow," said the pencil man. "Bring boots."

"I have boots."

"Then you'll need to decide."

He did not tell what the decision was. He didn't have to.

I rode home down the lane, which was silent, the fair behind me shining in my bones with its music. The Dandy under-hummed as though he was some sort of secret. I considered not becoming my street. The thought was not running away, it was a pulling away in a new direction.

When mum came to supper she enquired about the fair. I mentioned the lights and doughnuts, no more. Arthur said, "They come. They go." I shook and allowed him to think he had spoken seriously.

On this night I left the window open. The low throb of the generator was beating on the wind like a heartbeat that I knew now. I had a dream, the Noah's Ark, wood underfoot, wind in my face, the sensation of motion and being at the same time.

Before morning I had known two things, that I would go back again, and this time I would not be a spectator. The very evening I was standing on the road with a satchel on the shoulder and some lace boots tied, and the hum of the fair in the air, like a call. The pencil man noticed me through the lorry with his head tipped by the open door.

"On, then."

I climbed up. It began to start the engine, and to move the ground, and then the town--my trapped-up world--was starting to move in the wrong direction. I wasn't angry. I wasn't escaping punishment. I was taking a response to an invitation. And when the lights of the fair faded behind me I saw: I was not out of the corner. I just turned around and began to walk.

Here I must leave you now--in that first chapter, in which the paper rounds are yet unfinished and the BSA Dandy whistles its first note, in which the fair lights have not yet faded and the lorry door is half-open tomorrow.

Chapter 2 will continue the story-onward, by miles, errors, little favours, making paper rounds my passport that is stamped at the places I could not spell.

And in case you read this because you have been in your own corner--a literal or otherwise one, keep in mind: corners are what the room becomes; they are what show where it turns. It is the manner in which you make that turn; pull your head up, keep your breath steady, your hands on the throttle.

The road ahead is yours. Just keep moving.

Chapter 2
The Boxing Tent

Into the Lorry

The lorry door slammed behind me like a gate closing on everything I'd ever known. I stood on the running board a second longer than I should have, satchel over my shoulder, boots still warm from the lane. The pencil man (he told me his name was Reg, but nobody ever used it) just nodded toward the dark inside. "In you get, lad. Night's wasting."

The engine coughed itself awake and the fairground lights shrank to coloured pinpricks, then to nothing. I felt the pull in my stomach the same way I once felt it watching trains disappear. Only this time I was on the train.

Inside smelled of diesel, sweat, and fried onions long gone cold. Benches ran down both sides, crates lashed in the middle. A single bulb swung from the roof, throwing shadows that jerked like drunks. Men sat quiet, saving strength. One of them looked up, cigarette glowing under the peak of a flat cap.

"You the new lad for the joints?" I nodded. "Sit there. Don't touch nothing that ain't yours."

I wedged myself between sacks of coconut matting and tried to look smaller than I felt. The lorry lurched, gears grinding, and we rolled out past the Noah's Ark ride still turning to empty air, music fading behind us like a song you only half remember.

Hours later the bulb went out and the dark pressed in proper. I must have dozed, because the next thing was a boot nudging my leg.

"Wakey, English. You're home."

We'd stopped in a lay-by somewhere north. Dawn was a grey smear on the windscreen. The boxer was climbing down from the cab, tall, shoulders filling the doorway, hair black and brilliantined even after a night on the road. He looked twenty-four going on forty and twice as handsome as any man had a right to be.

"Tam McGraw," he said, sticking out a hand the size of a Christmas ham. "Glasgow. You'll be bunking with me. Try not to snore."

He laughed at his own joke, white teeth flashing, then turned and pissed against the back wheel like it was the most natural thing in the world. The others just stepped round him. I decided then and there I liked him.

The lorry we slept in was parked behind whichever showground we were working that week. Six of us in there: Tam, me, two Poles who spoke no English, a quiet lad from Cork, and an old man they called Professor who fixed the dodgems and never took his waistcoat off, even in bed. Bunks were two tiers, thin mattresses that smelled of every man who'd ever cried or wanked or died on them.

Tam had the top bunk above mine. First night he came in late, girl on his arm, both of them giggling. The others pretended to sleep. I lay staring at the underside of his mattress while the springs sang their old song inches above my face. When it finished he leaned over the edge, hair hanging down like a curtain.

"You awake, wee man?"

"Aye."

"Good. Tomorrow you'll see what proper money looks like."

He dropped something onto my chest. A ten-bob note, still warm from wherever it had been. "Welcome to the show," he said, and rolled back up into the dark.

I held that note a long time. It smelled of sweat and cheap scent and something I hadn't known I was hungry for: possibility. Outside, the generator thumped steady, like a heart that belonged to nobody and everybody. I listened to it until it lulled me under, the same way the trains once had, only now the rhythm was taking me away instead of reminding me I was stuck.

When I woke again it was to Tam shaking my shoulder. "Up, Michael Reed. Time to earn your keep."

Sun was bleeding across the field, turning the Waltzers into gold. I swung my legs down, boots hitting the floor with a clunk that felt like the first beat of a new song. I didn't know the words yet, but I knew the tune, and it went something like this: keep moving, keep listening, keep your fists ready. I was sixteen and the road had finally opened its mouth and swallowed me whole. And I was grinning.

Twelve-Hour Days and Midnight Pull-Downs

The days started when the sky was still the colour of a bruise and didn't finish until the stars looked close enough to touch.

We built the fair like an army on the march. Reg pointed, we ran. Joints to be bolted, boards to be hammered, cables thicker than my wrist dragged across mud that sucked your boots off if you stood still too long. My hands learned new aches: knuckles split from spanners, shoulders burning from hauling the dodgem track, palms blistered raw then hardening into something useful.

The boxing booth went up last, pride of place near the entrance. Red and gold canvas, hand-painted sign that read:

FIGHT TAM "THE GLASGOW HAMMER" McGRAW 3 ROUNDS – £30 IF YOU FLOOR HIM NO HEADGUARDS – NO MERCY

Tam stood on the platform in his vest, oil on his chest so the light caught it, shouting in that rich Glasgow roll. "Who's the man tonight, boys? Come on, big Englishmen, show me what you've got!" Men queued with their pints and their pride, rolling sleeves, wives shouting advice. Most lasted thirty seconds. One lasted two minutes and walked away with a broken nose and a story. None ever saw the thirty quid.

I worked the flap, took the money, handed out the gumshields. Between bouts I swept blood and sawdust, wiped the canvas with a rag that never came clean. The air inside the tent was thick: sweat, liniment, cigar smoke, the coppery tang of split lips. It got into your clothes, your hair, your dreams.

When the punters thinned out we still weren't done. Midnight on Saturday the generator coughed its last and the lights died one by one. Then came the pull-down.

Everything that had taken twelve hours to raise had to come apart in three. Men moved like ghosts under hurricane lamps, breath white in the cold. Spanners clanged, canvas flapped like gunshot, steel poles crashed to the ground hard enough to rattle your teeth. I learned to jump clear when the big top folds collapsed, learned the exact second to duck when the Waltzer cars swung free on their chains.

Tam worked harder than anyone. Shirt off, muscles shining with sweat even in November, singing old Glasgow songs while he wrestled king poles the size of telegraph masts. Once a pole slipped and came down like a tree. Tam shoved me clear, took the weight on his shoulder, roared until three others got under it. Afterwards he just laughed, lit a fag, and said, "See, wee man? That's why they pay me the big money."

By three in the morning the field was empty except for ruts and rubbish and the smell of trampled grass. We climbed back into the lorry, black with dirt, bones humming. Someone passed a bottle of Newcastle Brown. It went round until it was gone. Nobody spoke much. We didn't need to. The ache in our bodies said everything.

I'd fall into my bunk still tasting sawdust and adrenaline. Above me Tam's breathing would settle into the slow rhythm of a man who could sleep through anything. Sometimes a girl would climb in with him later, the springs creaking soft and steady, and I'd lie staring at the rivets in the roof, feeling the miles stacking up under the wheels even while we were parked.

Those weeks blurred. One town bled into the next: Dewsbury, Castleford, Workington, Barnsley. Same mud, same faces, same shouts of "Who'll take the Hammer?" Same midnight thunder of steel coming down. My hands turned into a man's hands without asking permission. My shoulders filled the seams of the old coat Mum had bought me two winters before.

And every Saturday night when the last light died and the field went dark, I felt it again: that same lift in the chest I'd felt the first time the BSA Dandy roared to life. Only now it wasn't a little 98cc engine under me; it was the whole bloody fairground, and I was part of the machinery that made it move.

I was tired to the marrow, bruised, filthy, richer by a few quid each week, and happier than I had any right to be. The road had its teeth in me now, and I didn't mind the bite one bit.

Sunday Roasts and Clean Shirts

Sunday morning the lorries rolled into the winter yard at the back of Retford, a patch of gravel and puddles ringed by caravans with smoking chimneys. The fair slept there one day a week, like a big beast catching its breath.

We lined up outside the pay caravan, caps in hand, mud still caked on our boots. The guv'nor's wife sat inside with a cashbox and a cigarette that never went out. Eleven pounds exactly, notes crisp and smelling of the bank. I folded mine into the same pocket that still held the smell of last night's canvas and blood.

41

Tam clapped me on the shoulder. "Roast dinner, wee man. Your ma still doing the good Yorkshire puddings?"

I nodded. She was.

We caught the local bus, the two of us smelling of diesel and hard work, sitting up top because the windows were cleaner. Tam had a carrier bag with his dirty washing; I had mine. Folk gave us room. We looked like trouble and Sunday best at the same time.

The village had changed while I'd been gone. New houses on the old rec, a telephone box where the bomb site used to be, and our new house (three bedrooms, inside toilet, a garden big enough for Dad to stand in without touching both fences). He'd left the railway, taken a job in the sugar-beet factory, steady money at last. Mum said the quiet was strange after all those years of trains.

Little Susan (my sister, born while I was still facing the wall at school) opened the door before we knocked. Seven years old, gap-toothed, fierce as a terrier. "Michael!" She launched herself at my legs. Tam swung her up like she weighed nothing, and she squealed loud enough to bring Mum running, apron on, eyes shining.

Elsie hugged me so hard I felt my ribs creak. Then she hugged Tam the same, because he was mine now, and that was the rule. Dad stood in the doorway in his slippers, nodding once, the way he did when words felt too big.

The kitchen smelled of beef fat and sage. The table was already set with the blue-rimmed plates saved for best. Mum had ironed our work shirts the week before and kept them hanging

42

in the airing cupboard; they came out warm and smelling of home.

We ate like men who hadn't seen proper food in a month. Roast potatoes crisp enough to break your teeth on, gravy thick as axle grease, Yorkshire puddings the size of hubcaps. Tam told stories between mouthfuls (Glasgow stories, hard men and soft hearts), making Mum laugh until she had to wipe her eyes with the tea towel. Dad listened quiet, cutting his meat into perfect squares, but I caught him smiling twice.

Afterwards Mum took the carrier bags and disappeared to the twin-tub. The machine thumped and sloshed like a slow heartbeat. Susan dragged Tam into the garden to show him her swing. Dad cleared his throat.

"You keeping out of trouble?"

"Trying, Dad." He nodded, eyes on the window. "Your mother worries."

"I know."

Tam came back in with grass on his knees and Susan riding his shoulders. He set her down gentle, then looked at Dad straight. "Your lad's a good worker, Mr Reed. Best pair of hands we've had in years." Dad didn't answer right away. Then he reached for the teapot, refilled Tam's cup without asking, and that was that.

Later, clean shirts on our backs, bellies full, we sat on the front step sharing a Woodbine. The sun was low and soft, the colour of Mum's apricot jam. Tam blew smoke rings and watched them drift.

"You ever think of stopping, Michael?"

"Stopping what?"

"This." He waved a hand at the sky, the road, everything.

"Fairground. Road. Fighting other men's fights for them." I shrugged. "It's movement."

"Aye," he said. "But movement's easy. Standing still's the hard part."

I didn't know what to say to that, so I didn't say anything. The bus back to the yard came round the corner, brakes hissing. We stood up, shirts tucked in, hair combed with water from the kitchen tap. Mum pressed a paper bag into my hand (cold beef sandwiches wrapped in greaseproof, two slices of apple tart).

"See you next Sunday," she said, and kissed my cheek quick so nobody would see the shine in her eyes. Tam lifted Susan one last time, then we were on the bus, waving through the back window until the village disappeared.

That was our rhythm for two years: six days of hammers and blood and midnight steel, one day of roast beef and clean shirts and the smell of Mum's kitchen clinging to our skin. It was the closest thing to family the road ever gave me.

And every Sunday night when the lorry pulled away again, I carried that warmth in my chest like a hot coal, enough to keep the cold out for another week. But nothing lasts forever. Not even Tam's smile, or the red-and-gold booth, or the sound of a crowd roaring for blood.

The Night They Banned the Booth

It ended on a wet Saturday in Keighley, the sort of night where the rain came sideways and the punters still queued because Yorkshiremen would rather drown than miss a fight.

The booth was packed, air thick enough to chew. Tam had already flattened four locals (one sailor with tattoos, two miners who'd had a skinful, and a cocky lad from Leeds who thought sideburns made him hard). Blood speckled the canvas like rust. I was wiping the ropes between bouts when the coppers pushed through the flap.

Six of them, helmets shining under the lamps, notebooks already out. The crowd hushed the way it only ever does when authority walks in wearing size-twelve boots.

"Show's over, lads," the sergeant said. "New by-law. No more bare-knuckle for money. Pack it in."

Tam stood in the ring, chest heaving, gloves hanging loose at his sides. Sweat ran pink down his ribs. He looked at the sergeant, then at the crowd, then at me. Something passed across his face I'd never seen before: the first shadow of being finished.

Reg argued, voice climbing higher with every sentence, but the coppers weren't in the mood for discussion. They started herding men out. Someone booed. A bottle smashed. Tam climbed down from the platform slow, like he was walking through water.

Outside, the rain hammered the canvas roof. We stood under the awning while the law watched. Tam lit a fag with fingers that shook only a little.

"That's it, then," he said, smoke mixing with the rain. "No more thirty quid for three rounds."

I didn't know what to say. The booth had been the loudest thing in my life for two years, and now it was just canvas and rope and a sign that would never be hung again.

We pulled it down in silence. No singing, no bottle going round. The king poles came down easier than they'd ever gone up. By three in the morning the field was empty except for puddles and the smell of wet sawdust. The other lorries had already gone. Ours was the last.

Tam slung his kitbag into the back, then turned to me.

"I'm off south, Michael. Pubs still pay for a decent tear-up. Police look the other way if the landlord's happy." He tried a grin, but it sat wrong on his face. "You coming?"

I looked at the dark field, at the ruts already filling with water, at the place where the ring had been an hour earlier. I thought of Mum's kitchen tomorrow, the smell of beef and the sound of the twin-tub. I thought of the eleven pounds in my pocket that suddenly felt like nothing.

"Nah, Tam. I'm done."

He nodded once, like he'd known the answer before he asked. Then he pulled me into a hug that cracked my back and smelled of liniment and Embassy Regal.

"You're all right, wee man. You'll land on your feet. You always do."

He climbed into a different lorry (some lads heading for Manchester, fights in back rooms and cellars) and the tail-lights disappeared down the road. I stood there a long time, rain soaking through my coat, until even the sound of his engine was gone. The yard next morning was half-empty. Reg handed me my wages and a week's notice rolled into one.

"Nothing personal, son. No booth, no crowd. Simple as that." I caught the bus south with my kitbag and the taste of sawdust still in my mouth. The villages slid past the window, same as ever, only now they looked smaller, as if the world had shrunk while I'd been away.

When I got off at our stop the street was quiet, Sunday-quiet. Mum opened the door in her pinny, eyes going wide when she saw me mid-week, alone, soaked to the skin.

"Michael?"

I dropped the bag in the hall and let her hug me. Dad stood behind her, saying nothing, just resting a heavy hand on my shoulder for a second. Susan peered round his legs, thumb in mouth. I smelled the roast already in the oven, heard the wireless murmuring, felt the warmth of the two-bar fire reach out like it had been waiting.

I was nineteen, skint, and suddenly on my own again. The road had spat me out. But I was home. And tomorrow was Monday, and Mondays always brought something (whether you were ready or not). I'd stood in corners before. I could stand in this one until the next door opened.

And somewhere inside me, the boy who once believed the world only moved past him finally understood: sometimes it stops, turns round, and waits for you to climb aboard again.

Chapter 3
Hearses and Hard Knocks

Back to Square One

The coach braked outside the village chippy on a Tuesday that felt like every other Tuesday I'd ever tried to escape, only this time I was coming back instead of going. Sky the colour of cold tea, rain spitting on the wind. Nineteen years old, eleven pounds folded in my pocket, kitbag over my shoulder smelling of sawdust, blood, and Tam McGraw's last Embassy Regal. The fair had shut its doors, the boxing booth was banned, and the road that had swallowed me whole two years earlier had spat me out again like a cherry stone.

Mum opened the door still holding a damp tea towel. Her eyes asked the questions her mouth didn't need to: Where've you been, what happened, are you all right? She answered them herself by pulling me over the step and holding on so tight I felt the last of the fairground shake loose from my ribs. Dad stood behind her in factory overalls, sugar-beet dust on the cuffs now instead of railway coal. He gave me the single nod he'd given the day I rode home on the BSA Dandy: you're here, lad. We'll manage.

Susan (my sister, seven going on seventeen) grabbed my sleeve and dragged me inside, words tumbling out about school, her new kitten Sooty, and how she'd kept my old bed even though she wanted the bigger room. The house smelled of shepherd's pie and carbolic soap and something I hadn't realised I'd missed until it hit me in the chest. They'd turned my old bedroom into hers, but the narrow iron bed was still squeezed into the box room under the eaves. I dropped the kitbag, sat on the springs that squeaked the same note they always had, and felt the quiet settle on me like a blanket too heavy to throw off.

Next morning, I walked the village looking for anything that paid. Same faces behind the same net curtains, same dogs barking behind the same gates, only now I was taller and the streets looked narrower. The garage on the main road had a piece of cardboard in the window: BOY WANTED. I pushed open the door smelling of last night's rain and old diesel.

Mr Parrish, the owner, was wiping hands on a rag that had once been red. "Know anything about cars?"

"Not much, but I'm quick."

"Start Monday. Seven bob an hour. Don't be late. And get a haircut."

Monday, I turned up in overalls Mum had boiled twice to get the fairground out of them. The other mechanics were grown men with wives, mortgages, and opinions about youngsters. They called me "college" because I was young and useless. I swept the floor, made tea thick enough to stand a spanner in, fetched spark plugs, and learned the smell of hot sump oil and Swarfega under my nails.

I was good with my hands. Always had been. Give me something broken and I'd tinker until it breathed again. After a year they let me near real jobs. I could strip a carburettor blindfolded, weld a patch so neat you'd swear the metal had never split. But when I asked about an apprenticeship Mr Parrish just sucked his teeth and said the board wanted school certificates, and I didn't have any to show.

Four years I stayed. Four years of being the best unpaid mechanic in the county, of coming home with hands black no matter how hard Mum scrubbed, of watching lads younger than me walk out with indentured papers while I swept the same floor. Then one Friday he called me into the office, handed me a brown envelope, and said trade was quiet. The envelope had three weeks' money and no argument.

I walked home past the chippy, past the same faces that now looked sorry for me instead of frightened of me. Twenty-one years old, back on the scrapheap with the smell of hot oil still in my nose and nowhere left to put the next foot. The corner I'd stood in at school felt very close again, only this time the wall was made of grown-up silence and there was no teacher to tell me when I could leave.

The Old Wedding Cars

Mr Parrish knew a man who kept a fleet of vintage limousines in a barn that smelled of mouse droppings, old leather, and the ghost of better days. Rolls-Royces mostly, a couple of Daimlers, all pre-war beauties hired out for weddings and funerals. Paintwork dulled by decades, chrome pitted like old teeth, engines seized solid with neglect and damp.

I spent my days in that barn with a welding torch, a tin of Brasso, and the patience I'd learned pulling down fairground rides at three in the morning. I coaxed life back into them one by one: a 1936 Phantom III that coughed like an old smoker then settled into the smoothest purr I'd ever heard, a Silver Ghost whose winged radiator cap looked ready to take flight again, a Daimler whose seats still held the shape of long-dead lords and ladies. Mr Caldwell, the owner, watched me get the Phantom running one afternoon, pipe glowing in the gloom like a tiny red eye.

"You drive as well, lad?"

"I drove a motorbike before I could spell the word."

"Start tomorrow. Uniform's hanging in the office. And mind you polish the shoes."

First wedding was in June, warm enough for confetti to stick to everything. Bride nervous as a kitten, veil trembling in the breeze, father sweating through his morning coat and trying to look proud. I held the door of the Silver Ghost, cap peaked, gloves white as Sunday best. The bride smiled at me in the mirror all the way to church and I felt taller than the car itself, taller than the church spire.

Funerals were different. Black Daimler, curtains drawn, twelve miles an hour exactly so the coffin didn't shift. Old ladies in black hats pressed a shilling into my palm afterwards and called me a good lad. I pocketed the coins and never told them I was the same boy who once stood in a classroom corner because letters wouldn't stay still.

I liked the work. Liked the hush of a country churchyard, the smell of polished walnut and old leather, the way the big cars glided like ships on a calm sea. Liked that nobody asked if I could read the road signs; they only cared that I got them there on time and in one piece. For a year I thought this might be the thing that stuck.

Weddings paid better. Bridesmaids giggled in the back, drunk on nerves and Babycham, skirts riding up over stockinged knees. Fathers shook my hand and slipped me a crisp fiver. Once a groom was so nervous he was sick behind the lychgate, and I lent him my clean handkerchief. His new wife kissed my cheek and left lipstick the colour of danger.

Funerals were quieter, heavier. I learned to keep a spare clean hanky in the glovebox for widows who cried all the way to the cemetery. Learned to slow down for corners so the flowers didn't slide. Learned the exact weight of silence when the curtains closed and the family walked away across the grass.

I was twenty-one, driving cars older than my dad, wearing a peaked cap and a tie that felt like borrowed respect. Mum ironed the shirts until they could stand alone, Dad polished my shoes on Saturday nights with spit and elbow grease. Susan thought I was a film star and begged for rides in the Rolls. I let her sit in the back once, just round the village, and she waved at her friends like the Queen.

Then one Tuesday Mr Caldwell took me into the office that smelled of pipe tobacco and bad news. Petrol prices up, people choosing modern cars, fewer weddings, fewer funerals worth dressing up for. He shook my hand, pressed a ten-pound note into it like a full stop, and said sorry, son.

I walked out of the barn for the last time with my overalls over my arm and the smell of polished leather clinging to my skin. Twenty-two years old and on the scrapheap again, only this time the scrapheap had chrome bumpers and the ghosts of brides who'd long since stopped smiling.

I stood in the lane outside the barn and felt the old corner pressing in, only now it was made of grown-up silence and the smell of lilies left too long in water. I'd learned to stand still once before. I could do it again. But not for long.

Asbestos and the Little House

I took what I could get: stripping asbestos from old factory boilers and pipework in buildings nobody wanted any more. The money was rubbish, but it was money, and it came every Friday in a little brown wage packet that felt heavier than it had any right to.

We wore paper suits that tore if you breathed too hard, masks that steamed up so you couldn't see your own hands, gloves thick as oven mitts. The dust got everywhere anyway: in your hair, your ears, the creases of your neck. At the end of the day you stripped naked in a porta-cabin, shoved your clothes into a bin bag, and showered until the water ran grey. Even then you could taste it at the back of your throat, like chalk and metal and something that might kill you thirty years later.

I worked with men who'd been doing it since the war. They coughed like dogs and called me "college" again because I was the youngest. I learned to cut lagging with a bread knife, to wet it down so the fibres didn't fly, to stuff the wet grey mess into plastic sacks that weighed more than Susan. My hands blistered, then hardened, then blistered again.

53

Every Friday I walked to the estate agent's window and stared at the same little terraced house on Inkerman Street: two-up two-down, cracked panes, a yard you could cross in three strides. Three thousand quid. I stood there so often the woman inside started nodding hello.

One Friday the asbestos money, the last of the hearse tips, and a bit I'd saved from the fairground all added up. I walked in, put the cash on the counter in a biscuit tin because I didn't trust banks, and said I wanted the house. She counted it twice, raised an eyebrow at the tin, but took it. The keys were cold and heavy in my palm.

I moved in with a second-hand bed that sagged in the middle, a cooker that worked three rings out of four, and a kettle I'd bought Tam a lift with once. Mum came round with curtains she'd run up on her Singer, floral ones that made the place feel less like a cave. Dad brought a hammer, nails, and a tin of paint the colour of custard. Susan carried the kitten in a cardboard box and christened every room with a sneeze.

We had beans on toast for tea off a packing case and it tasted better than any wedding breakfast I'd ever seen. That night I lay in my own bed under my own roof and listened to the house tick itself cool. No trains, no generator, no Tam breathing above me. Just quiet, and the smell of fresh paint, and the feeling that maybe I'd finally stopped falling.

I kept stripping asbestos. Kept banking every penny. Then a proper job came along: two weeks refitting pipework in a big mill that was closing down. Good money if I finished on time. I worked sixteen-hour days, hands raw, back screaming, living on sandwiches and tea that tasted of dust.

When it was done, I phoned the woman who'd hired me. She said bring the invoice Monday. Monday, she locked the gates while I stood outside with my tools and my mouth open.

"Gone bust, love. Receivers took everything. Nothing left."

I stared at the padlock that might as well have been on the moon. Months of graft, gone. I crossed the road to the pub because my legs wouldn't take me anywhere else, sat on a stool, and told my story to the bar towel because it was softer than people. The pub was almost empty. One man at the far end nursed a pint, oil-skinned coat dripping on the floor. He listened to me finish, then slid a fresh beer across without asking.

"Same thing happened to me in '72. Lost three months overnight."

"What did you do?"

"Went north. Oil rigs. They're crying out for lads who aren't afraid of hard work or heights." He wrote a telephone number on the back of a fag packet and pushed it over.

"Aberdeen." I stared at those seven digits until the barman turned the lights up for closing time. The little house was mine, but the mortgage still had to be paid and the cupboards were bare. Next morning, I caught the coach north, kitbag on my knee, biscuit tin empty under the seat, and the taste of asbestos still at the back of my throat.

I was twenty-three, owned four walls, and was running again. Only this time I wasn't sure what I was running from or what I was running to. Just knew the road was moving under me once more, and I'd learned long ago never to stand still when it did.

The Man with the Number

The coach north took twenty-three hours of breakdowns, cold tea, and service-station sandwiches that tasted of cardboard and regret. I sat with my kitbag on my knee, staring out at motorways and moors sliding past in the dark, the fag packet with the Aberdeen number folded tight in my fist. Every mile felt like another page ripping off the calendar of the life I'd been trying to build.

When we finally rolled into Aberdeen bus station the air smelled of salt and fish and something sharp I couldn't name yet. Gulls screamed overhead like they owned the sky. I found a phone box that still had glass in the windows and dialled with my last ten-pence piece.

"Personnel. Speak."

"I've come from Nottinghamshire. Twenty-three hours on a coach. Looking for work."

Long silence.

"No jobs, son."

"I've come twenty-three hours." Another silence, then a sigh that sounded like the sea itself.

"Come to the office anyway."

The personnel man sat behind a desk piled with clipboards and coffee rings. He looked like he'd eaten nails for breakfast and spat rust. The interview was a disaster. I knew nothing about rigs, nothing about drilling, nothing about the North Sea except it was cold and wet.

"What can you actually do?"

"I'm young. Strong. I learn quick. I've welded, driven, worked nights, worked heights on the fair. I don't scare easy."

"That's not enough out there." I opened my mouth and God alone knows what made the words come out. "Well, I've watched Dallas on the telly. Does that count?"

He stared at me a second, then barked a laugh so loud the secretary poked her head round the door. "Christ, lad, if you've seen Dallas you're probably more qualified than half the buggers we've got. Most of them think J.R. Ewing runs the whole bloody North Sea."

He scribbled an address on a chit and handed me a taxi voucher. "Medical tomorrow morning. Pass that and we'll put you on the next crew change."

I passed. Lungs clear, heart strong, eyes good enough. Two weeks later I was back in Aberdeen, standing on the quayside watching helicopters lift off like angry green wasps, blades chopping the air into pieces. Men in red coveralls and hard hats queued for the crew boat, faces burned brown by wind and sun even though it was February.

I had forty pounds in my pocket, a new pair of steel-toecaps Mum had bought me, and the smell of the little house still on my skin. I thought of Mum's face when I told her I was going offshore (proud and terrified in the same breath), of Dad's quiet nod, of Susan waving from the front step with Sooty in her arms.

I thought of the boy who once stood facing a classroom wall because letters wouldn't stay still, and I near enough laughed out loud. That boy was about to climb into a helicopter and fly fifty miles out to sea to work on a platform taller than any building he'd ever seen, doing a job he couldn't spell, for money he couldn't count yet.

The crewman tapped my shoulder. "Reed? You're on this one." I shouldered my kitbag and walked up the steps onto the helideck. The rotors spun faster, the noise swallowed everything (thought, fear, yesterday). I strapped in beside men who looked like they'd been born in hard hats. The chopper lifted, stomach dropping, Aberdeen shrinking to a grey smudge, then nothing but water.

I pressed my forehead to the cold window and watched the North Sea rush up to meet us. Somewhere under those waves men were pulling oil out of the dark, and I was going to be one of them. The corner was a long way behind me now, and the wall had turned into sky. I was grinning like an idiot, and nobody told me to stop.

Chapter 4
Aberdeen, 23 Hours

The Yard of Hard Men

The helicopter dropped us on a supply boat that stank of fish and hydraulic oil, then we motored out to the rig like a cork bobbing on a grey washing-up bowl. When the platform finally rose out of the mist it looked impossible (steel legs thicker than houses, flares burning orange on top, the whole thing standing on the sea as if God had hammered it there and walked away). I was twenty-three and had never felt smaller.

They flew me back to Aberdeen two days later for the survival course, but the real education started the moment I stepped through the gate of the shore base yard on my first proper shift.

The place was a sea of mud and drill pipe. Thousands of thirty-foot joints stacked like giant Meccano, all needing cleaning, checking, painting. The yard foreman was a Scot built like a public toilet (broad, red-faced, and smelling of last night's whisky). His name was McAllister, but nobody used it; he was just "the Gaffer" or, when he wasn't listening, "that bastard."

Thirteen men waited ahead of me for an offshore seat. Thirteen Scots in donkey jackets and steel-toecaps, all older, all harder, all waiting weeks already. I was the only Englishman. They looked at me the way cats look at a new dog.

First morning the Gaffer handed me a wire brush and pointed at a mountain of pipe. "English, you're on rust. Move it."

I moved it. Twelve hours a day, seven days a week, scraping rust that came off in red snow, paint that stank of benzene, cold that went straight through gloves. My hands split, scabbed, split again. The Scots sang in Gaelic just loud enough for me to know it wasn't friendly.

Then one Tuesday another Englishman turned up (big lad, soft round the edges, rosy cheeks, nervous smile). The Gaffer took one look and started in.

"Look what the cat dragged in. Another English bastard. You lost, fatty?"

He poked the lad in the belly with a broom handle. Then again. Then kicked his shin. The new lad (his name was Terry) went white but said nothing. After an hour he muttered he had to go to the office and walked out. The Gaffer laughed so hard he had to lean on a pipe.

Ten minutes later Terry came back in the back of a police car, pointed through the window, and said in a voice that shook only a little, "That's the man that assaulted me."

Two constables climbed out. The Gaffer's face went the colour of corned beef. The American yard manager (big Yank in a hard hat and mirrored shades) appeared like a genie somebody had rubbed the wrong way.

The police gave the Gaffer an official warning: touch the lad again and you're nicked. The Yank didn't say a word, just stared until the Gaffer looked at his boots.

Next day the Gaffer was back at it, only now he kept his hands to himself. Terry was brushing rust two pipes away when the Gaffer started shouting, "You stupid English twat, can't you even—"

He never finished. A huge articulated lorry had pulled into the yard to deliver casing. The driver (English, built like a brick shithouse, forearms like hams) heard the word "English" and jumped down.

"What did you just fucking say?"

The Gaffer opened his mouth. The driver punched it shut. One punch. The Gaffer dropped like a sack of spuds.

The Yank came storming out again, face like thunder. "Goddamn it, what the hell is going on now?"

The driver explained, calm as you like, that the Gaffer had just called him an English bastard and an English twat. The Gaffer, sitting in the mud with blood on his chin, tried to say he'd been talking to himself. The Yank turned to his English secretary who'd followed him out.

"Which ones are English?"

Me and Terry raised our hands.

"Right," the Yank said. "You two are offshore tomorrow morning. Get them sorted."

The Scots started moaning (three months we've been here, etc.), but the Yank just walked away. The Gaffer sat in the mud and didn't say another word.

That night I shook Terry's hand and the driver bought us both a pint in the pub round the corner. I slept in a cheap B&B with the sound of the sea in my ears and the taste of tomorrow on my tongue.

Twenty-three hours on a coach, one punch in a yard, and the North Sea opened its gates. I was going offshore. And I was grinning again.

First Flight Out

The helicopter lifted off Aberdeen heliport at half past five in the morning, still dark enough for the town lights to look like a handful of dropped coins. I sat strapped in beside Terry, both of us in brand-new red coveralls that still smelled of the packet, life-jacket tight across the chest, ear defenders clamped so hard my head throbbed. The rotors thundered, the deck fell away, and my stomach stayed behind for a second before catching up.

Below us the sea was black glass, broken only by the white wake of supply boats and the occasional flare stack burning like a match held to the night. Fifty miles out, maybe sixty (far enough that land was a rumour). The pilot's voice crackled in the headphones: "Ten minutes to touchdown, gentlemen. Welcome to the real world."

The rig grew out of the water like something built by giants in a bad mood. Legs thick as gasometers, decks stacked on top of each other, flare boom spitting fire that lit the clouds orange. It looked impossible, brutal, and beautiful all at once.

We came in fast, wind rocking the chopper like a toy. The deckhand waved us down, one hand on his hard hat, the other giving the pilot the finger for fun. Then the skids kissed steel and the noise dropped to a roar you felt in your teeth.

A roustabout in a beard and a grin unclipped me. "English? You'll do. Follow the yellow footprints, don't fall off, don't puke on my deck."

I stepped out onto the helideck and the wind hit me like a slap. Salt and oil and hot metal. The whole platform vibrated with pumps and generators and men shouting over them. Someone shoved a hard hat on my head, another clipped a tag to my coveralls: ROUSTABOUT – REED.

They marched us down steel stairs that rang like church bells. Every level smelled different: diesel, coffee, wet rope, frying bacon. Men passed going the other way (some nodding, some blank, some looking like they'd forgotten what sleep was). One old boy with a face like a crumpled map stopped Terry.

"First trip, fatty? Don't eat the curry. Trust me."

Terry went pale. I laughed, because someone had to.

The toolpusher (big Geordie with arms like dockyard cranes) met us in the mess. "Right, you two English heroes. You're on the drill floor tomorrow, but today you're paint and grease monkeys. Move your arses."

We spent the day chipping rust the size of dinner plates, painting over it with red lead that stank and stuck to everything. My hands turned the colour of raw meat. The wind never stopped; it came straight off the Arctic and went straight through you. By knock-off at six I was shaking with cold and tired enough to cry, only I didn't know how any more.

The mess room at supper was a steamy cave of noise and clattering trays. Steak pie, chips swimming in gravy, tinned peas hard as bullets. I ate three platefuls and still had room. Terry sat opposite me, face grey, pushing food round.

"You all right?"

"Feel sick."

"Drink some milk. And stay upwind of the curry."

That night I lay in a bunk the size of a coffin, earplugs in, the whole rig rocking gentle on the swell. The steel walls hummed. Somewhere a pump thumped like a slow heart. I thought of the little house on Inkerman Street, of Mum's curtains, of Dad's quiet nod, and then I didn't think of anything at all because sleep took me like a blackjack to the head.

Next morning at five the lights snapped on and a voice bellowed, "Wakey wakey, ladies, the world's still turning!" I swung out of the bunk, feet hitting cold steel, and realised I was grinning again. The boy who once stood in a corner because letters danced was now fifty miles out to sea, about to start his first proper shift on the drill floor of a North Sea oil rig.

I pulled on my coveralls, still damp from yesterday, and followed the smell of bacon and danger down the corridor.

The sea was waiting, and so was the money.

And for the first time in my life, I felt exactly the right size for the job.

The Drill Floor

They put me on the drill floor after one week of chipping and painting. One week was all it took for the toolpusher to see I wasn't afraid of heights, noise, or getting my hands dirty. "Reed," he said, spitting tobacco juice into a bucket, "you're roughneck material. Don't die."

The drill floor was hell with the lid off.

Forty feet above the sea, open on three sides to the wind, everything slick with drilling mud the colour and consistency of chocolate pudding. The derrick towered another hundred and fifty feet above us, pipes hanging in it like organ pipes in a mad church. The rotary table spun with a roar that lived inside your bones. Every few seconds the travelling block (four tons of steel) thundered up and down on cables thick as my wrist.

My first trip as floorman I stood on the monkey board eighty feet up, wind trying to peel me off the derrick like a sticker. Below me the crew screamed over the noise, hand signals flashing: thumbs up, fist to helmet, two fingers spinning. I learned fast because the penalty for learning slow was a pipe in the face or a one-way trip into the North Sea.

The crew were wild men. Half the Americans were fresh out of Vietnam or fresh out of prison (sometimes both). One driller from Louisiana had a tiger tattooed on his chest and a laugh like a chainsaw. Another roughneck, a Scot called Jock, could bend a six-inch bolt with his bare hands when he was drunk, which was often. They called me "English" or "Pretty Boy" and tested me every shift: sending me for the long weight, the left-handed spanner, a tin of tartan paint. I fetched everything with a straight face until they ran out of jokes.

I slipped pipes with the best of them, spun chain like I was born to it, cleaned mud pits until my back screamed. Twelve hours on, twelve off, two weeks straight. Hands bled, scabbed, bled again. I lost two stone and grew muscle I didn't know names for. The money was obscene (more in a fortnight than I'd earned in a year stripping asbestos), paid into a bank account I didn't know how to read.

One night the sea turned nasty. Waves hit the legs so hard the whole rig shuddered like a wet dog. We were tripping pipe (pulling a mile of steel out of the hole) when the rig lurched and a joint swung wild. Thirty foot of drill collar scythed across the floor straight at Terry. I grabbed his harness and hauled him clear; the pipe missed us by inches and smashed into the stump. The toolpusher saw it, spat, and said nothing. Next day my pay slip had an extra hundred pounds "danger money". I sent half home to Mum without a note. She knew.

When the two weeks ended they flew us back to Aberdeen in weather that made the pilot swear in Gaelic. I walked off the heliport with salt crust on my skin and more money in my pocket than I'd ever seen. My hands shook when I tried to light a cigarette, not from fear any more, but from the engine still running inside me.

I checked into the same cheap hotel near the docks (ten quid a night, shared bathroom, smell of fried onions and despair). That night three girls checked in (black girls from a tiny village in Devon, someone said). They wore short skirts and big smiles and didn't ask for money. Word went round they were carrying something in body cavities, but nobody asked questions when the lights were low. I lay awake listening to the headboard next door thumping like a slow pump and thought: this is the life now. Danger, money, women who appear and vanish like smoke.

Next morning, I queued for the survival course (four days of freezing water, lifeboats, fire training). I jumped from a thirty-foot platform into a tank so cold it stopped my heart for a second, then started it again harder. I passed. They gave me a certificate I couldn't read and a handshake that cracked my knuckles.

I was twenty-four, roughneck, offshore-certified, and owned a house I hadn't seen in a month.

The boy who once stood in a corner because the letters danced was now dancing with the devil on a steel island in the middle of the North Sea, and the music was getting louder. And I hadn't fallen off yet.

Coming Down to Earth (For a Bit)

The survival course finished on a Friday. They handed us our certificates and a rail warrant home, and suddenly the noise stopped. No rotors, no klaxons, no generators thumping through the night. Just Aberdeen rain on the window of the train south and a quiet so loud it hurt my ears.

I walked into the little house on Inkerman Street at half past ten on a Saturday morning. Mum was at the sink, sleeves rolled, radio murmuring. She turned, saw me standing there in rig coveralls and a face full of salt and sun, and dropped a plate. It didn't break. She was across the kitchen before it hit the floor, arms round my neck, crying into my shoulder like I'd come back from the dead.

Dad came in from the garden, took one look, and did the nod (only this time it was slower, deeper, like he was measuring something). Susan ran in, screamed "Michael!" and climbed me like a tree. Even Sooty the cat rubbed against my oily trousers as if I still belonged.

I had four weeks off. Four weeks of money in the bank, of sleeping in a bed that didn't move, of eating Mum's roast dinners until my ribs creaked. I bought Susan a new bike, paid another chunk off the mortgage, took Dad to the pub and watched him try not to look proud when the barman asked what my lad did for a living.

But the quiet started to itch.

One morning a neighbour mentioned a mate who'd done an HGV course (five days, a hundred quid, proper ticket). I walked down to the training school that afternoon, still tasting North Sea salt at the back of my throat, and signed the form. Five days of clutch control, reversing round cones, and learning which gear made the engine sing instead of scream. I passed first time. The examiner shook my hand and said, "You drive like you're running from something." I laughed and didn't tell him I was running toward it.

Getting a start wasn't easy (no experience, they all said). I knocked on every depot from Nottingham to Newark, got told no so often the word stopped meaning anything. Then Manpower Services rang: two weeks driving a flatbed for the council, then straight onto an agency that fed the rigs. Two weeks offshore earning silly money, two weeks on the road earning decent money (same employer, different worlds). They called it the "slash rotation": 2-and-2. I called it perfect.

First lorry job was hauling aggregate to a site outside Lincoln. The cab smelled of cigarettes and air-freshener trees, the radio played Tammy Wynette, and the road unrolled in front of me like a promise. I sat high above the cars, gears slotting smooth, air horns blaring at boys who waved from bridges. For the first time since the fairground lorry I felt the old lift in my chest: movement again, only now I was the one in the driving seat, literally.

I'd come home from a rig trip with a pocket full of wages, climb straight into the lorry cab the next morning, then four weeks later reverse the journey (lorry to chopper, chopper to rig). Two lives stitched together with diesel and avgas. Mum stopped asking when I was going to settle down; she just kept the kettle on and the fridge full.

One Sunday night I stood in the back yard of the little house, smoking a last fag before the early flight north. The sky was clear, stars sharp enough to cut yourself on. Somewhere out there past the horizon the rig flares were burning, waiting for me. Somewhere behind me the village slept under its old roofs. I owned a house, a heavy goods licence, and a job that paid more in a month than Dad had earned in a year on the railway.

The boy who once believed the world only moved past him now moved the world (or at least shifted tons of it at a time, by road and by sea).

I flicked the cigarette into the dark, watched the dot of red arc and die. Tomorrow the chopper would lift me above the clouds again, and the noise would start all over: rotors, pumps, men shouting, money stacking up like pipes in the yard. I was twenty-four, roughneck, lorry driver, homeowner, and still running. Only now I knew exactly where I was running to. And I couldn't wait to get there.

Chapter 5
Roustabout

The First Real Trip

The alarm went at four-thirty, a klaxon that sounded like the end of the world. I swung out of the bunk still half-dreaming of home, feet hitting cold steel before my eyes were properly open. Red coveralls, still damp from yesterday, clung to my legs. The corridor outside was already alive (boots clanging, voices thick with sleep and Geordie curses, the smell of bacon and wet wool drifting up from the galley).

Breakfast was a stampede. I piled my plate with eggs fried solid, sausages black as drill pipe, and beans that could patch a hull. You ate fast because the chopper waited for no man's digestion.

By five-fifteen we were on the helideck, wind whipping the breath out of your mouth, rotors already turning. The North Sea was gunmetal grey, white horses galloping across it like they had somewhere better to be. I strapped in beside Jock the mad Scot and Terry (who'd slimmed down and toughened up until nobody called him fatty anymore). The chopper lifted, banked hard, and Aberdeen fell away beneath us.

Seventy miles out this time, further than I'd ever been. The rig appeared first as a red glow on the horizon (the flare stack burning off gas like a dragon with indigestion), then grew into the biggest thing I'd ever seen built by men. Four hundred feet from sea to heliport, legs thicker than the cooling towers back home, decks stacked like a mad wedding cake. The name painted on the side in letters ten feet high: SEA QUEST.

We touched down in a storm of spray and noise. A deckhand grabbed my harness the second the door slid open. "Reed! You're late, ya English bastard. Move!"

I was late by exactly thirty seconds and grinning like an idiot.

They put me straight on the drill floor crew (permanent now, no more yard waiting). My station was the monkeyboard, eighty-five feet up the derrick, clipped on with a belt that felt flimsy as string. Below me the rotary table roared, mud pumps thumped, and the pipe racked back so fast it whistled. My job: catch each thirty-foot joint as the derrickman kicked it out, ride it into the rack, latch it home. One slip and you fed the sea.

First connection of the shift we were tripping in (running new pipe into the hole). The driller, a Texan called Ray who'd lost two fingers in Vietnam and grown them back meaner, gave me the nod. The travelling block came screaming down, pipe swinging like a pendulum. I reached, caught the bail, felt the weight try to rip my shoulders out, and slammed it home. The latch clanged shut. Ray looked up, gave me one slow nod, and that was better than any pay rise.

Twelve hours later, my arms were jelly, and my ears rang like church bells. I climbed down the derrick ladder one careful rung at a time, legs shaking, hands too sore to grip. In the changing room I peeled off gloves crusted with mud and blood and saw my palms were raw meat again. Jock clapped me on the back hard enough to stagger me.

"Welcome to the crew, English. You'll do."

That night I lay in my bunk listening to the rig breathe (pumps thumping, generators growling, the sea slapping the legs far below). Everything hurt in a clean, honest way I'd never known before. I had a permanent bunk now, my name stencilled on the locker: M. REED. I ran my fingers over the letters and felt something settle inside me, something that had been restless since the day I first faced the classroom wall.

I was a roustabout turned roughneck, earning more in a week than Dad had in a month on the footplate. I owned a house, a heavy goods licence, and a future that didn't depend on school certificates or teachers who thought I was thick.

Out the porthole the flare stack painted the clouds red and gold. Somewhere under us men were drilling three miles into the earth's crust, pulling up black gold that would change the country. And I was part of it (small part, greasy part, replaceable part), but part of it all the same.

I fell asleep with the taste of salt and diesel in my mouth and the certainty, for the first time in my life, that tomorrow would be louder, harder, and better than today. And it was only the first day.

Men Who Came Back from the Dead

The crew I joined was a collection of men who'd already used up most of their luck and were borrowing the rest. Half the

Americans had Vietnam stamped on them like a brand you couldn't see but could smell (cigarette smoke, jungle rot, and something sharp behind the eyes). The other half had prison tattoos and stories they only told when the whisky was gone and the North Sea was black outside the windows.

Ray, the driller, ran the floor like a sergeant major with a hangover. Forty-two years old, two fingers missing from a mortar round in '68, voice like gravel dragged across steel. When he said "Jump," you didn't ask how high; you were already in the air. He'd scream at you one minute and hand you a cold Coke the next without changing expression. I learned more from Ray in a month than I'd learned in four years of garages and hearses.

Then there was Big Davie from Glasgow (six-foot-six, fists like hams, heart bigger than the rig). He'd done time for glassing a man in a pub fight and come out smiling. Davie taught me how to throw the chain so it wrapped the pipe like a snake, how to read the driller's hand signals when the noise swallowed voices, how to laugh when a wave hit the rig so hard the coffee jumped out of your mug.

And there was Terry (my fellow Englishman who'd started fat and frightened in the yard). Two trips offshore had burned the fat off him and replaced it with wire and gristle. He still spoke soft, but now when he said "Move" men moved. We shared a cabin, swapped stories about home, and never once mentioned the day the Gaffer went down in the mud.

The work never let up. Twelve hours on, twelve off, but the twelve off were eaten by sleep, food, and the endless small jobs that kept the beast alive. You painted when you weren't pulling pipe, greased when you weren't painting, cleaned mud tanks that stank like the devil's armpit. One shift I spent four hours in a space so tight my shoulders touched both walls, welding a patch on a tank while breathing through a hose because the air would kill you otherwise. When I crawled out I was black from head to toe and shaking like a dog, but the weld held and Ray slapped my back so hard I saw stars.

The money rolled in faster than I could count it. I sent half home every trip (Mum cried the first time a thousand pounds arrived in the post). The rest went on tools, boots, and the occasional mad night in Aberdeen when we came off the chopper with two weeks' pay burning holes in our pockets.

Those nights were legend. We'd hit the docks pubs (places with sawdust on the floor and names like The Prince of Wales and The Broken Oar). Whisky flowed, fights started over nothing, and girls who liked roughnecks appeared like magic. I woke once in a boarding house with a tattoo of an anchor on my forearm and no memory of getting it. Mum saw it when I went home and just shook her head, smiling.

But the sea gave nothing for free. One trip we lost a derrickman (good lad from Peterhead, slipped on ice ninety feet up, fell straight past the monkeyboard into the drink). The search went on for hours, helicopters circling, boats cutting white scars in the black water. They never found him. Ray stood on the drill floor afterwards, stared at the spot where he'd been standing, and said quiet, "That's the price, boys. Pay attention." We all paid attention after that.

Yet every morning when the klaxon screamed and I climbed the derrick in the dark, wind trying to rip me off, I felt more alive than I ever had facing a classroom wall or sweeping a garage floor.

I was twenty-four, roughneck, earning wages that made grown men blink, living with men who'd stared death in the face and laughed. And every time the travelling block thundered past my ear and I latched another pipe home, I felt the old corner shrink a little further behind me. The North Sea was trying to kill us, and we were too busy living to care. And the best shift of my life was still coming.

The Night the Rig Caught Fire

It was the middle of a black February night, three o'clock in the morning, the kind of cold that gets inside your bones and sets up home. I was on the back shift, twelve hours of tripping pipe out of a hole that didn't want to let go. We were all knackered, covered in mud, dreaming of the bunk and a brew.

Then the alarm went off: not the usual wake-up klaxon, but the long, rising howl that means one thing only: fire.

Every light on the rig snapped red. The tannoy crackled: "Fire in the pump room, fire in the pump room. All hands to emergency stations."

I was out of the monkeyboard and down the ladder so fast my boots barely touched rungs. Men poured from every hatch, pulling on breathing gear, faces white under the helmets. Ray was already on the drill floor, roaring orders like we were still in a jungle clearing instead of a steel island seventy miles from anywhere.

The pump room was below the main deck, a maze of pipes and valves and diesel. Something had sparked (nobody ever found out exactly what) and the whole place had gone up like a box of matches. Flames licking thirty feet high, black smoke rolling out thick as tar.

We formed a human chain with fire hoses, passing them hand to hand because the pumps were part of what was burning. The heat hit you like a wall. Paint blistered on the bulkheads. I remember thinking, clear as day: this is it, this is how it ends, roasted alive for a pay cheque.

Ray grabbed me by the harness. "Reed! You and Davie, get the foam monitor round the back. Move!"

Big Davie and I dragged the heavy hose through corridors already filling with smoke. My throat burned, eyes streamed, but we got the monitor in place and let it rip. White foam shot out like a snowstorm, smothering the flames nearest the accommodation. The noise was unreal: roaring fire, screaming metal, men shouting over it all.

Terry appeared beside us, face black, dragging another hose. He looked at me once and grinned the mad grin we all had that night. We were terrified and alive and doing something that mattered.

It took two hours. Two hours of heat and smoke and praying the tanks didn't go up. When the last flame died the rig looked like a battlefield: hoses everywhere, foam dripping from the rails, men on their knees coughing their lungs up. The sea around us was calm, almost gentle, as if it hadn't noticed we'd nearly burned our home down.

Ray walked the floor afterwards, checking every man. When he got to me he just put a hand on my shoulder and squeezed once. No words. None needed.

We lost the pump room, half the pipe deck, and two fingers off a lad from Dundee who'd tried to shut a valve with his bare hand. But we saved the rig. Saved the accommodation, saved the helideck, saved every soul aboard.

At knock-off the sun came up red over a sea flat as glass. I stood on the pipe deck with a mug of tea that tasted of smoke and stared at the damage. My hands shook so badly I spilled half of it. Davie came and stood beside me, huge and quiet.

"You did good, English."

"We all did."

"Aye. But you didn't run."

"Where was there to run to?"

He laughed then, a big Belfast laugh that shook the morning, and slapped my back hard enough to rattle teeth. That trip they gave every man on the fire party an extra five hundred pounds danger money and a week's leave when we got ashore. I sent most of it home again. Mum bought a new three-piece suite with hers and never told Dad where the money came from.

I flew home with soot still under my fingernails and the smell of burning diesel in my hair. When the chopper landed at Aberdeen I looked back once at the horizon where the rig sat like a scarred boxer, still standing, still flaring.

I was twenty-four, roughneck, fire-fighter, and I'd stared into the mouth of something that could have killed us all and helped shut it.

The corner was a long time ago now, and the wall had turned into fire. And I was still standing on the right side of it.

The Letter from Home

The trips blurred into one long roar of steel and sea, money and muscle. Two weeks on, two weeks off, lorry cab to chopper to rig and back again. My body hardened into something I didn't recognise in the mirror: shoulders wide as a door, forearms thick with rope-burn scars, hands that could bend pennies for a laugh. I was twenty-five, owned my house outright, and had more in the bank than Dad had earned in twenty years on the railway.

Then one morning in the mail room on the rig (a metal cupboard that smelled of coffee and wet paper), the steward handed me a letter in Mum's handwriting. The envelope was thick, the kind she used when there was news too big for a postcard.

I took it out to the smoking area on the pipe deck, wind whipping the flame off my lighter three times before the fag caught. The flare stack painted the sky orange behind me. I slit the envelope with a thumb that still had yesterday's grease under the nail.

Inside was a single sheet and a photograph. The letter was short. Dad had been taken poorly (chest pains, hospital, tests). The doctors said it was his heart. He was home now, resting, but he wasn't to go back to the factory. Mum didn't say "come home," but the words were there between every line. The photograph was Dad sitting in the new three-piece suite, thinner than I'd ever seen him, holding a cup of tea like it weighed a ton. Susan stood behind him with her arm round his shoulders, trying to smile for the camera and failing.

I read it twice, then folded it small and put it in the top pocket of my coveralls, right over my own heart. That shift I worked like a man trying to outrun something. I slipped pipe so fast Ray told me to slow down before I killed someone. When the klaxon went at six I didn't go to the mess. I went to the radio room instead and put in a call to the beach. The radio man patched me through to the little house on Inkerman Street.

Mum picked up on the second ring. "It's me."

"Michael." Just my name, and her voice cracked on it. "How bad is he?"

"He's awake. He's breathing. But he's frightened, love. And he won't say it."

"I'm coming home."

"You've got a job—"

"I'm coming home."

I signed off the rig the next morning. Ray shook my hand without a word and slipped an extra envelope into my pocket (two weeks' danger money he said the company owed me anyway). Big Davie hugged me so hard my feet left the deck. Terry just nodded once, the way men do when words are too small.

The chopper lifted off at dawn. I looked down at the rig (my steel island, scarred and flaring and still standing) and felt something shift inside me. I was going back to the village, back to the little streets, back to a house with floral curtains and a man who'd never once told me he was proud but had shown it every day in quieter ways.

I didn't know how long I'd stay, or whether the North Sea would let me leave for good. All I knew was the letter in my pocket weighed more than any pay cheque I'd ever cashed.

When the chopper banked south and the rig disappeared behind us, I pressed my hand to the window and made the rig a promise I wasn't sure I could keep.

I'll be back. Because some fires don't go out just because you walk away from them. And some men are built for the heat.

Chapter 6
Sand in My Boots

Waiting Rooms

I landed in Dubai late in the evening, tired enough that the heat felt like someone opening an oven door straight into my face. A man from the company held a card with my name on it. He didn't say much, just pointed me towards a white minibus with the air-con whining like it was about to die.

The company had put me in a four-star hotel near the airport. From a distance it looked grand enough—glass front, polished steps, big chandelier in the lobby—but the moment I pushed through the doors, the truth hit me. The bar was wall-to-wall working girls. They leaned on the railings in bright dresses, laughing, smoking, eyeing up anyone who looked like they had a wallet. It wasn't subtle. I'd barely checked in before three of them asked if I wanted "company." I said no, took my key, and went up to the room.

The company told me I'd be in the hotel for "a couple of days" before my visa for Iran was sorted. It turned into five. I hate waiting. I'd worked all my life, done nights in the cold and the rain, welded gear in storms, and dragged drilling pipe in temperatures you could fry an egg on. But sitting in a hotel room, day after day, with nothing to do—that's its own kind of punishment. It felt like being stuck in a holding pattern, circling with no place to land.

Each morning I'd go downstairs, nod at the receptionist, get the same story: "Nothing yet, sir." Then I'd take the lift back up, lie on the bed, stare at the ceiling fan, and wonder what I'd let myself in for. The girls in the bar worked around the clock. Half the roughnecks and expats took them upstairs. The whole place felt like a waiting room for men going somewhere they weren't sure they'd come back from.

On the fifth day my visa came through. They rang my room at six in the morning and told me I'd be flying out that afternoon. They gave me a ticket and a small brown envelope with my deployment papers. Simple as that. No briefing, no explanation. Just "off you go."

The flight to Kharg Island—the Iranians call it Karg—was full of oil men. Most of them didn't talk. They had the look of people who'd seen enough to know that saying nothing was safer. I'd been told Karg was one of the most bombed places in the world. Hard to imagine until you see it from the air: scorched patches, twisted metal, rusted skeletons of old installations. No green anywhere. Just dust, concrete, and the sea.

By the time I landed, the company had changed hands again. It had already gone from Loffland Brothers to Nabors, and now it was KCA Drilling. Every time they changed owners, the rules changed with them. Different paperwork, different priorities, different people to keep happy. It always meant trouble down the line.

A driver met me and John—the driller who'd come in on the same flight—and took us out to where the rig was supposed to be. We drove past blown-out buildings, half-buried machinery, and rows of shipping containers that looked like they hadn't moved in years. We stopped at a patch of dirt with a few men standing around smoking. No rig in sight.

John looked at them, then at me.

"Where's the rig?" he asked.

One of the Iranian crew shrugged.

"Rig coming," he said.

"When?"

Another shrug. "Soon."

That was the welcome.

They took us to the accommodation block. I'd seen bad places before, but this one made the fairground bedsit look like a hotel. Filthy walls, cracked tiles, brown water out of the tap. The air-con didn't work. The mattresses were thin enough to fold in half with one hand. I dropped my bag on the floor and sat on the edge of the bed. You could smell damp, sweat, and something chemical.

The food was worse. First night I tried the stew. Within an hour I was doubled over. It wasn't just me. Everyone had the same problem—constant trips to the toilet, day and night. It didn't take me long to find out that the crew from Total had their own dining hall. Clean, proper food, proper hygiene. I started eating with them whenever I could slip in. No one stopped me. They probably felt sorry for us.

After a few days I learned the unspoken rules.

Don't drink the water.

Don't trust the food unless you see it boiled.

Don't leave your boots outside the door.

Don't expect equipment to arrive on time.

Don't argue with the local foremen; it'll only make things worse. And don't ask too many questions about the past—you won't like the answers.

I'd worked in rough places before, but Karg felt different. There was a weight to it, like the ground still remembered every bomb that had ever hit it. You could feel it under your feet. I didn't know it then, but this was only the start of what would be the hardest posting of my life.

Pieces of a Rig

The next morning, John and I walked out to the same patch of dirt where the Iranian crew had been standing. Still no rig. Just heat, dust, and a few bored-looking men leaning on crates. One of them waved at us like we were late for a party no one wanted to attend.

About an hour later, we heard engines. A convoy of old lorries came crawling along the track, each one stacked high with rusted steel, pipes, cables, and bits of machinery held together with rope. This was our rig—or what was left of it. It looked like someone had taken it apart with a hammer and hoped for the best.

John sighed.

"So that's it."

I nodded. "Looks like it."

They parked the lorries in a line. The drivers jumped out and walked off without a word. No paperwork, no instructions. Just dumped it and left. The Iranian toolpusher gave us a smile like this was completely normal.

We walked around the piles of metal, trying to make sense of what went where. I'd built rigs before, but never from something that looked like it had been dragged through a scrapyard. John kicked at a piece of twisted steel.

"Four months," he said.

"What?"

"That's how long this'll take."

He wasn't wrong.

We started working straight away. The days blurred into each other—long hours, searing heat, dehydration creeping up on you until you realised you hadn't pissed all day. We didn't have half the gear we needed. Everything was late, broken, or missing. When we asked for replacement parts, we were told they were "on the way." That phrase became a joke. Everything was always "on the way." Nothing ever arrived.

During those months, the company changed hands again. Now it was officially KCA-Deutag. Same logo slapped on the paperwork, same confusion, different managers who had no idea what we were actually dealing with. Each change meant new forms, new rules, new people from head office flying in to tell us how to run a rig they'd never seen.

We built that rig bolt by bolt, weld by weld. Some days the wind blew sand so hard it felt like needles against your skin. Other days the air stood still and you worked in heat heavy enough to make you dizzy. We drank warm water out of plastic barrels and tried not to think about where it came from.

The Iranian crew kept mostly to themselves. Good men, hard workers, but wary. They had seen too many foreigners come and go, promising big things and delivering nothing. They watched us, testing us with small tasks first. When they saw we weren't afraid to get dirty, they eased up.

Our accommodation didn't get any better. The toilets flooded twice. The shower only worked on odd days. We shared rooms with cockroaches the size of matchboxes. I learned to sleep with earplugs so I didn't hear them scuttling over the floor at night.

Most evenings I walked to Total's mess hall, blending in with their lads. Their food wasn't amazing, but at least it didn't send you running to the toilet. One of their cooks started saving me a plate under the counter, pretending he didn't see me coming in through the wrong door.

One night, sitting outside with a warm can of cola, I heard distant rumbling. At first I thought it was thunder. Then I saw lights streaking across the sky—bright trails cutting through the darkness. They looked like shooting stars.

John came running out of his room.

"You see that?"

"Yeah."

"Those aren't stars," he said. "Those are missiles."

He was right. They were tomahawks, fired from American ships across the water. They arced silently overhead, vanished beyond the horizon, and a moment later, the sky flickered with a faint glow. No sound. Just light. It was like watching the world blink.

The next morning the Iranian toolpusher acted like nothing had happened. Business as usual. That was when I realised this wasn't a place where people talked about danger. They lived with it, the same way you live with bad weather or long winters. It was part of the job.

After about four months, the rig finally took shape. It wasn't pretty, but it worked. The first time we powered up the draw works, it groaned like a dying animal, then steadied. We all stood around looking at it like we'd just raised the dead. John patted the side of it.

"Not bad," he said. "For scrap."

We started drilling a week later. H_2S alarms went off so often you stopped reacting. We wore breathing apparatus half the time. Some of the older German supervisors from the Deutag side of the company wandered around telling us how it should be done while having no clue what they were looking at. Half the time I was doing their work for them just to keep things moving.

But the well was going down. Slowly, painfully, but down.

And with the drill turning, the reality settled in: I was stuck here, on this battered patch of rock in the Persian Gulf, working for a company that changed names more often than it changed filters, surrounded by danger that nobody acknowledged.

This was survival, plain and simple. And I was learning the rules, whether I liked them or not.

Learning the Edges

Once the drilling started, the days fell into a rhythm—if you could call it that. Nothing about Karg felt steady. The ground shook sometimes, just tiny tremors left over from old bombs or maybe from the plant a few miles away. No one explained anything. If you asked, the answer was always the same: "Normal."

The first week of drilling nearly finished us. The bit kept hitting pockets of gas. Every few hours, the H_2S alarms screamed, and we'd grab our gear, masks tight, eyes watering from the chemical sting even through the filters. The Iranian lads moved fast. They'd done this before. Some of the Germans stumbled around looking confused, arguing in broken English about pressures and flow rates while the rest of us were just trying to stay alive.

Most nights I sat in my tiny room, boots still on, listening to the ceiling fan rattle like it was about to fall off. I'd wipe the dust off my face with a wet rag and try not to think too much. If you thought too much about this place—about the heat, the gas, the distance from home—you'd tie yourself in knots. I focused on the job. That was the only way through anything.

One thing became clear early on: KCA-Deutag didn't have a clue what was really happening out here. They sent emails about "efficiency" and "workflow compliance" while we were trying to stop gas from blowing through the stack. One manager in a clean shirt flew in one afternoon, walked around for twenty minutes, nodded at nothing, and left again. He didn't even see the flare pit. When the helicopter blades lifted off, the Iranian toolpusher spat on the ground.

The crew started trusting me more once they realised I wasn't afraid to get my hands dirty. The Germans weren't much help, so I handled most of the night operations myself. Night shifts are different. There's no sun burning your neck, but the darkness has its own weight. You hear everything—the groan of the derrick, the hiss of gas, the creak of a cable ready to snap. Your mind goes to strange places when the only light is a few bulbs and the glow from the flare.

I learned small tricks to stay alive. Keep a spare mask close. Always check your boots for scorpions. Don't stand near the flare if the wind changes. And never, ever take your eyes off a gauge for more than a second. The well doesn't care who you are. It'll kill you just as quick whether you're a rookie or the most experienced hand on the pad.

The Iranian drill crew were tough men. One of them, Hamid, barely spoke English but had eyes like he'd seen every kind of disaster. He could tell when a kick was coming just by the way the mud line trembled. He taught me things without saying a word—hand signals, nods, small taps on a valve. Working with him made the nights feel less like a gamble.

We ate together when we could. Their food was simple— rice, flatbread, stewed meat—but far better than the slop in our own mess. They laughed more than we did. Maybe you have to laugh if you've spent half your life on a rock that everyone keeps bombing. One night one of them pointed to an old crater near the accommodation block and said, "I was sleeping when that one came." Then he just shrugged, like that was a normal part of life.

One afternoon a dust storm rolled in so fast the sky turned orange in seconds. We had to shut everything down and hold the rig steady. The wind howled through the derrick, shaking the whole structure. Sand came through every crack in the cabin. For a moment I thought the mast might topple. John stood beside me, both of us bracing against the vibration.

"We're not paid enough for this," he muttered.

"Try telling them that," I said.

When the storm passed, everything was coated in a layer of grit. We had to clean out every filter, every line, every bit of machinery. It took hours. You could taste sand in your teeth for days afterward.

A few weeks later, another small reminder of where we were arrived—a distant thud, then another. Not loud, but deep, like someone dropping a wardrobe in the next building. The Iranian crew didn't react. They didn't even look up. I realised then that on Karg, explosions were no different from weather changes.

As the weeks turned into months, I felt myself adjusting to the place. Not accepting it—just learning how to live along the edges without getting cut. The trick was not letting the fear grow roots. Fear is fine when it's small. It keeps you awake. But if you feed it, it becomes something else.

The rig crept deeper into the formation. Systems steadied. The nights felt less frantic. I still didn't trust the company, but I trusted the work, and sometimes that was enough to keep going. Karg didn't get easier. You just got used to the weight of it.

The Quiet Rules

By the time the well reached its first proper section, the chaos of those early weeks had settled into something that almost felt like routine. Not safe—never safe—but predictable in the way dangerous places sometimes become. You start recognising the patterns. When a gauge twitches, when a pump sounds wrong, when a man hesitates for half a second longer than he should. You build a sense for trouble before it lands on your shoulder.

The company sent out a new supervisor from KCA-Deutag. He arrived in a clean shirt and shiny boots that barely touched the dirt. He walked around with a clipboard, asking questions that proved he didn't understand what any of us were actually doing. John answered him politely; I didn't bother. Men like that never stayed long. They came out, ticked boxes, wrote reports, and flew back to air-conditioned offices where the biggest risk was spilling coffee on a keyboard.

The Iranian crew kept everything running. I'd started taking my breaks with them, sitting on overturned buckets in the shade, drinking tea so strong it tasted like copper. They didn't talk much about the past or the politics. What mattered was the job and the small agreements that kept everyone alive. They had their own hierarchy, quiet but strict. Once you understood who listened to who, the whole place made more sense.

One evening I walked to the mess and found the food worse than usual—grey meat, overcooked rice, no flavour. Half the lads were already sick again. I turned around and went straight to the dining hall used by Total. Their security man at the door gave me a look, but he'd seen me enough times to know I wasn't trouble. The cook handed me a plate without a word. That was another unwritten rule on Karg: take care of the ones who turn up every day and don't make life harder than it already is.

Nights were the worst. The wind carried strange noises—metal shifting, machinery cooling, the sea slapping against the rocks. Sometimes I'd sit outside my room and watch the flare burn against the dark. The glow bounced off the sand and made the whole island look like it was lit from underneath. You could almost convince yourself the ground was alive.

One night, Hamid sat beside me. He didn't speak for a long time. Then he pointed toward a line of broken concrete in the distance.

"Bomb," he said. "Long time ago."

I nodded.

He tapped the ground with his boot. "Still here."

That was Karg. Everything that had ever happened stayed in the soil, in the metal, in the way the men looked at the horizon. You weren't just working on a rig. You were living on top of history that had been blown apart more times than anyone cared to count. By the end of that rotation, I'd learned enough to survive. Not thrive—just survive. Know when to speak, when to shut up, when to look the other way, and when to stand your ground. Know who to trust. Know what to eat. Know which alarms mattered and which ones were just another reminder that nothing on this island ever really slept.

When the helicopter finally came to take me off Karg for my days off, I felt the blades whipping the heat around us and thought one thing: If this was only the beginning, God help me for what was coming next.

Chapter 7
Building Giants from Scraps

Four Months of Steel and Heat

When you build a rig from the ground up, you learn very quickly what's real and what's just the company brochure. Out here on Kharg Island, nothing matched the photos. The rig parts we'd been given looked like they'd been dragged out of a ditch and thrown onto lorries by men who wanted nothing more to do with them. No instructions, no proper inventory, nothing labelled. Just heaps of steel in every shape except the one you needed.

Once the first well started to turn, you'd think the chaos might ease up a bit. It didn't. If anything, the pressure got worse. We weren't just keeping the place running—we were still building half of it with whatever we could salvage. Every day meant crawling over machinery that had sharp edges, missing guards, bolts that didn't belong where they'd been hammered in. We had to tighten everything twice, test it three times, and hope the bloody thing didn't tear itself apart when we spooled up.

One morning, not long after we spudded the well, a fresh group of supervisors arrived from KCA-Deutag—older German lads mostly, brought in because the company had merged again and wanted "standardisation." They stepped off the helicopter in spotless overalls, carrying briefcases. Briefcases. On Karg. I nearly laughed.

They walked around the rig floor like tourists at a museum, pointing at equipment they clearly didn't understand. One of them, a tall fellow with silver hair, stood beside me near the mud pumps and said, "Zis is not correct procedure."

I asked him what procedure he was talking about. He flipped through a manual like he was reading a recipe.

I didn't bother arguing. There was no point. Half their instructions didn't apply to a rig built out of parts older than some of the crew. I'd spent months sweating into this metal, bolting it together while sand blinded us and H_2S alarms kept going off like a chorus. There was no manual for this thing. We were the manual.

John handled the Germans better than I did. He'd nod, smile, and then quietly tell the Iranian crew to do it the proper way. We all respected the Iranians by then. They were the backbone of the whole operation—steady hands, eyes that could see danger long before anyone else, and a kind of patience that came from living on a bombed-out island most of their lives.

Hamid showed me how to watch the mud return flow without staring at the gauges. "Listen," he said once, tapping the side of the metal tank. "Mud talks." He wasn't wrong. After a while you could hear when something wasn't right. A change in vibration, a hitch in the pump rhythm, a hiss where there shouldn't be one. Out here, sound kept you alive.

The heat was relentless. Some days it rose off the steel like fire. You couldn't touch anything without a glove, and even then you'd feel the burn. I drank so much water I stopped keeping count. Sweat dried on your clothes before it even formed. When the wind picked up, it carried dust straight into your mouth, grinding between your teeth until you tasted metal.

We worked to exhaustion because there was no other choice. When a rig is half-built and half-running, there's no rest. Everything is a risk. Every valve, every clamp, every section of pipe has the power to end your day or your life. It's not fear that gets to you—it's the responsibility. You're holding the whole bloody operation together with decisions you make every five minutes.

The German supervisors kept sending their reports back to headquarters, criticising things they didn't understand. They'd say the layout was wrong, or the equipment wasn't arranged according to their diagrams. They didn't grasp that we weren't working with a factory-fresh package. We were building a giant from scraps, fighting the climate, the terrain, the gas, and the clock.

One-night shift, John came into the doghouse looking fed up.

"What now?" I asked.

"One of the Germans wants us to re-route the choke manifold because it doesn't match the schematic."

I stared at him. "Does he know this rig wasn't built in the same decade as his schematic?"

"No."

"Then tell him to piss off."

John grinned. "Already did."

As the weeks dragged on, you could feel the strain in everyone. The Iranian crew's faces showed it most—dark circles, cracked hands, shoulders slumped with fatigue. But they kept going. They didn't complain. They'd seen harder times.

At night I'd sit outside the accommodation block and stare at the horizon. The flare lit the sky orange. You could hear distant machinery from other sites, humming like a low drone. If you didn't think about the danger, it almost felt peaceful— until the next alarm shrieked and pulled you back into reality.

Four months. That's what John had said when the rig arrived in pieces. He wasn't far off. We were building something massive with almost nothing, and every day it felt like we were one mistake away from losing it all. But we kept building. Because that's what you do. You build the thing in front of you, no matter what shape it comes in.

The Gas, the Germans, and the Grind

Once the rig was turning steady enough that we weren't expecting it to fall apart every five minutes, the next enemy made itself known properly—H_2S. We'd had pockets before, but now the deeper we drilled, the worse it got. Some days the alarm went off so often it felt like part of the soundtrack. A shrill scream, a red light, everyone grabbing masks, checking seals, looking around to see who'd frozen or panicked. Nobody admitted fear, but you could see it in the eyes. Gas doesn't care how tough you are. It'll drop the biggest man in seconds.

The Iranian lads were sharp with it. They didn't wait for instructions. They trusted their instincts and the signs the well gave off. I learned more from watching them handle a gas kick than I ever learned from any training course. Hamid would catch my eye sometimes, nod once, and we'd move valves together. No words. No time for them.

The Germans were a different story. They wandered around with clipboards, arguing over numbers while the rest of us were trying to keep the well from blowing. One of them—Karl, I think—insisted on checking every line against a procedural document he carried like a bible. He'd wave it at us mid-crisis.

"Zis is not how we do it in Deutag!"

I told him, "We're not *in* Deutag. We're on a rock in the Gulf, mate. Put the bloody book down."

He didn't. He just looked offended and walked off like I'd insulted the family name. Meanwhile, I had Iranian roughnecks covered in sweat and grit working twice as hard as any imported supervisor. They were the ones keeping the place upright, not the paper-pushers flown in from head office.

The worst of the gas hit one night around two in the morning. I remember it because everything went dead silent just before the alarm. That kind of silence isn't normal on a rig—something always hums or rattles. When it stops, you know it's bad. The pump tone dipped, the mud return changed colour, and Hamid shouted something in Farsi. Then the siren went off.

Masks on. Gloves tight. The whole drill floor felt like it was holding its breath. H_2S has a way of grabbing the back of your mind, making you wonder whether every inhale will be your last. We stabilised flow, bled pressure, and chased the kick down. Took nearly an hour. I didn't take my mask off until the toolpusher gave the nod.

Karl came out afterward asking why we hadn't followed a section of the emergency protocol exactly as written. I looked at him, still dripping sweat, and said, "Because if we did, you'd be in a bag right now." He didn't speak to me for two days after that.

Around the same time, the heat ramped up. It was the kind of heat that didn't just sit on your skin—it got inside your bones. The steel on the rig floor was so hot you could smell rubber soles melting if someone stood too long in one place. The Iranian lads soaked rags in cold water and tied them around their necks. It helped for about five minutes before turning warm again.

Water became its own problem. The supply the company brought in tasted like plastic and rust. You couldn't drink from taps unless you wanted to spend half the day in the toilet. I learned to stash sealed bottles under my bunk, away from the sun. The German supervisors complained about the water quality to management, who replied with a three-line email saying it was "within acceptable limits." That told me everything I needed to know about acceptable limits.

Once a week, we'd get a break long enough to sit down and eat without rushing. That's when I'd slip off to the dining hall used by Total. They never turned me away. I'd sit with whichever engineers or staff happened to be around and eat food that didn't look like it came out of a bin. They didn't care that I wasn't one of theirs. Maybe they understood that when you're drilling on Karg, everyone's in the same boat whether they work for the same company or not.

One evening on the walk back, John said, "We'll never be paid enough for this."

I said, "We're not paid enough, full stop."

He laughed, but there wasn't much humour in it.

The grind continued. Equipment failed, sandstorms hit, Germans argued, Iranians endured, and we worked. Every day chipped a little more off your patience. Every night you lay on the thin mattress listening to the island creak and groan under the weight of its own history.

We weren't heroes. We weren't special. We were just men trying to keep a badly assembled rig alive long enough to reach target depth. And somehow, day by day, we kept it going.

Holding the Line

As the well got deeper, the pressure climbed with it. You could feel it—not just through the gauges, but in the air on the rig floor. A kind of tension that settled in your muscles, making every movement sharp. We were drilling into territory that had no interest in cooperating. The mud weight had to be adjusted every shift. A bit too heavy and we risked fracturing the formation. Too light and the well would start kicking again. It became a constant balancing act, like walking a tightrope with your eyes half-shut.

The Iranian mud engineers were as tough as they came. They lived inside that mud pit room, shirts soaked through, faces streaked grey from dust. One of them, Reza, always had a cigarette tucked behind his ear. I don't think I ever saw him actually smoke it—it was just part of him. He'd scoop mud with a tin can, swirl it in his hand, sniff it, and tell you what was happening downhole as if the stuff spoke to him. He didn't need the fancy sensors or the Germans' charts. He trusted experience more than technology.

The Germans didn't like that. They preferred numbers. They'd stand around with their laptops, running simulations that had nothing to do with the real conditions we were dealing with. Karl once told Reza he shouldn't "handle samples like that." Reza nodded politely, walked away, and did it exactly the same way the next day. Because he was right. And the Germans weren't the ones who'd be first to die if the mud weight went wrong.

The heat didn't make life easier. By noon the metal handrails burned your palms through your gloves. Every step on the rig floor felt like standing too close to a fire. We drank constantly, but still ended shifts feeling like we'd been baked dry. Some days men fainted. Not from weakness—just from the simple fact that human bodies aren't meant to operate in that kind of temperature. The company said they were "monitoring the situation." I doubted that meant anything.

Then came the sandstorms. They didn't blow in gently. They attacked. One minute the sky was clear, the next it was a wall of brown rushing at us, swallowing the horizon. We'd scramble to shut down whatever equipment could be shut down. Sand got into every moving part—pumps, bearings, threads, your teeth, your ears. It scraped across the rig like claws. The storm hit so hard the derrick lights disappeared. You could stand a foot away from someone and barely see their outline.

We huddled in the doghouse, listening to the wind batter the steel. The Germans complained about "environmental hazards" like they'd discovered something new. John sat with his boots up on a crate, arms folded, looking like a man who'd already accepted that this was just life now. I sat beside him, watching the door rattle.

"You ever get used to this?" I asked.

He shrugged. "You don't get used to it. You just get tired of caring."

When the storm passed, everything outside was layered in dust. The whole rig looked like it had aged ten years in an hour. We spent half the next shift cleaning grit out of the machinery. Some parts were ruined. Others we managed to patch together because we didn't have replacements. The Germans wrote a report saying "preventative maintenance was insufficient." I told Karl he could prevent whatever he liked from the comfort of a distant office. He didn't reply.

One part of Karg that kept me grounded was the sea. On the rare quiet evenings I'd walk to the shoreline. The water looked still, but you could hear the distant hum of tankers, engines carrying across the dark. The lights from offshore platforms dotted the horizon like stars. If you ignored the gas alarms, the heat, and the shifting politics, it almost seemed peaceful. Almost.

But the island had a way of reminding you where you were. One night, while I was sitting near the rocks, I heard a low thud. Not thunder. Something deeper. The kind of sound you feel before you hear. The Iranians didn't react—they knew what it meant. Somewhere inland, probably near an old storage site, something unstable had gone up. Maybe leftover munitions, maybe a tank that hadn't been emptied properly. On Karg, explosives were just part of the landscape. Not threats. Just reminders.

Back on the rig, the tension rose again when we hit a stubborn patch of formation. Drilling slowed to a crawl. The bit chewed and scraped, refusing to bite properly. Torque spiked. Vibration rattled up the drill string. Every shift turned into troubleshooting—adjust weight on bit, tweak RPM, adjust mud viscosity, listen for changes. You didn't trust the equipment. You trusted the crew. And they trusted you back.

Late one night, Hamid tapped my shoulder and pointed to a faint tremor in the drill line.

"Shaker not happy," he said.

I listened. He was right. The sound was wrong—subtle, but wrong. We shut things down just in time. A weld had sheared on one of the supports. If we'd kept running, the whole shaker table could've torn free. Could've taken someone with it.

We repaired it with what we had. Not the right parts. Just metal, sweat, and stubbornness. By the end of that rotation, it felt like we weren't just drilling a well—we were holding back the entire island with our bare hands.

The Breaking Point

By the fourth month the cracks were starting to show—not just in the rig, but in the men. You can only live in tension for so long before something gives. Even the Iranians, usually steady as stone, were moving slower. Shoulders hunched, tempers thin. Not angry, just worn down in that quiet way men get when they've carried too much for too long.

The Germans looked worse. They weren't built for this place, not really. You can't train a man to handle heat that feels like it's peeling the skin off your face, or sand that grinds into your eyelids. Karl in particular had gone from lecturing everyone to pacing around with a hollow sort of stare. His clipboard was still in his hand, but he'd stopped writing in it. I think the island had beaten him, the same way it beat machinery—slowly, but relentlessly.

And that was before the blowout preventer started giving us trouble. It hadn't failed, not yet, but it was groaning in a way nobody liked. The BOP stack had been cobbled together earlier in the project, using whatever we could salvage. Half the bolts were mismatched. Some seals looked like they should've been retired years ago. It was holding, but only just.

One morning during checks, John crouched down beside the BOP control panel and said, "This thing's on its last prayers."

I didn't bother sugar-coating it. "We all are."

The company—whatever name it had that month—said replacements were coming. They were "on the way." Everything important was always "on the way." Parts, pay, support, safety gear. All on the way. None of it here.

One evening, after a long shift, I walked to the dining hall run by Total and found the usual guard at the door. He didn't smile, but he stepped aside. That was his version of a warm welcome. Inside, it was cooler—not cold, but not the blast-furnace heat of our accommodation. I ate quietly with their technicians, grateful for a meal that wouldn't send me running to the toilet. No one asked questions. It was a simple unspoken agreement: if you made it here, you'd earned your plate.

Back on our side, the mood on the rig was shifting. You could sense something brewing. Maybe it was the drilling pace slowing again, or the gas readings creeping up, or just the strain of too many long days stacked on top of each other. There was an edge in the air.

It snapped on a night shift.

The standpipe pressure jumped suddenly, climbing faster than it should. Reza was on it immediately, shouting for us to back off the weight. The alarms blared. Mud splashed up the flowline in thick surges. John was already at the choke control, moving like he'd been fired out of a gun. Karl burst into the doghouse shouting about shutting everything down by procedure.

"Not now!" John barked.

It wasn't a kick yet, but it could turn into one if mishandled. We steadied the pumps, adjusted the choke, and waited. The rig seemed to hold its breath with us. The pressure finally settled, like something angry had backed down—for now.

Karl threw his hands in the air.

"You ignore safety protocols!"

I stepped toward him. "You want protocols? Go sit at your laptop. We're keeping you alive."

He left, red-faced, muttering. But he didn't argue again for the rest of the shift.

After things calmed, I climbed up to the monkeyboard just to get away from the noise. From up there, the island looked unreal—dusty, cracked, and somehow still shimmering in the heat. The flare from the refinery far off glowed against the night like a burning eye. The air smelled of salt, gas, and something metallic.

Hamid came up the ladder after me. He didn't speak at first. Just stood beside me, hands resting on the railing, staring out.

"This place..." he said finally, shaking his head a little, "it takes from everyone. You, me... island does not care."

"No," I said. "It doesn't."

He smiled, but it wasn't a happy one. "We keep it together. But not forever."

He was right. All of us felt it. Something had to break—equipment, men, or the well itself. You could only run on fumes for so long.

The breaking point came quietly.

Two days later, after a scorching afternoon shift, Karl walked up to the toolpusher with his clipboard under his arm and said he was done. Finished. Wanted a seat on the next chopper off the island. No argument, no theatrics. Just a man who'd reached his limit.

And as he walked away, I realised I didn't blame him. Karg Island wasn't a place you just endured casually. It ate at you. It took pieces of you you never realised were available to take.

By the end of that rotation, I felt emptied out in a way I'd never known before. Physically exhausted, mentally scraped clean. But the rig was still standing. Stubborn, ugly, patched-together—and still drilling. We all were.

Chapter 8
The Island That Breathed Fire

The Night Everything Changed

You could work on Karg for months and think you understood the place. You didn't. None of us did. The island had a way of showing you a new face just when you thought you'd figured out its temperament. Sometimes it was a sandstorm. Sometimes it was gas. And sometimes it was something far worse — something alive beneath the surface, waiting for the right moment to make itself known.

My rotation had just ended. I'd flown back to Dubai for a few days' rest, though "rest" wasn't the right word for Dubai in those years. It was all mirrored towers, traffic fumes, heat that bounced off the pavement like a slap. I walked through the airport, already thinking about my next hitch on Karg, when my phone went off. A message from one of the lads on the island. *"Something's happened. Bad one."*

That was it. No details. No context. Just a knot in my stomach tightening. I called back, but the line was patchy. All I caught was noise, shouting, and then one clear sentence before the call died. *"Explosion at the refinery. Big one."*

Karg Island wasn't just our rig. It was pipelines, storage tanks, chemical works, and an entire refinery complex — old, tense, and stitched together with whatever Iran could keep alive under sanctions. It was a patchwork system: rusting pipes feeding older pipes, valves no one trusted, tanks that had seen too many summers. One spark in the wrong place could do what decades of bombs hadn't managed.

I got the full story later. It started as a small fire in one of the processing units. Nothing dramatic. The sort of thing the Iranians saw all the time and handled without fuss. But then something failed — a crude line, maybe; or a relief valve. Nobody was sure. What was certain was that pressure built somewhere it shouldn't have. And then it let go.

The blast ripped through the refinery like a hammer. Men were thrown off their feet. Windows shattered miles away. The sky lit up orange — so bright the lads on our rig thought daylight had come early.

By the time I got the second call, I was already booking the next flight back into Iran. I couldn't sit in a hotel in Dubai while the island burned. The company didn't object. They needed bodies. They always did when things went wrong.

When the helicopter dropped me back onto Karg, the air tasted different — heavy, smoky, with that bitterness you get from burning crude. Heat shimmered across the ground. Even far from the refinery, you could feel the aftermath humming through the soil. John met me at the pad. He looked older. Not in years, but in the eyes.

"You picked a hell of a time to come back," he said.

"What's the damage?"

"You'll see."

We rode in a battered Hilux across the island. The refinery loomed ahead like a wounded animal — blackened towers, scorched tanks, twisted metal still steaming in places. Fire crews were everywhere, hoses spraying down smouldering sections. The blast had torn open a storage pit, sending oil spilling out in thick, dark sheets.

The Iranian workers moved like men possessed. No panic, no hysteria. Just grim determination. Some were covered in soot, others with bandages on their arms or heads. A few had burns. None stopped working.

"They lost men," John said quietly. "More than they'll admit."

I nodded. That was the way here. Death wasn't reported. It was absorbed. We stopped near a section of collapsed piping. A man in a heat-stained uniform waved us back from a smoking crater. The ground around it was peppered with shrapnel — bits of metal still glowing faintly from the heat. You could hear hissed warnings in Farsi as they tried to isolate whatever was still live.

"How close did this get to us?" I asked.

"Too close," John said. "If the wind had been different, gas could've drifted toward the rig. Could've taken the whole place with it."

I didn't say anything. There wasn't anything to say. On Karg, danger didn't knock. It kicked the door in.

As we drove back toward the accommodation camp, the sky turned a sickly yellow. Smoke rose in thin columns across the island. The flare at the refinery was still burning, but dimmer — as if the island was trying to catch its breath. The whole place felt bruised.

That night I sat outside my room, watching the glow from the refinery flicker. The air smelled of diesel, burnt metal, and something chemical I couldn't name. The ground vibrated gently under my boots. Whether it was machinery or the echo of the blast, I couldn't tell.

Hamid joined me after a while. He sat quietly for a long time before speaking.

"Island angry today," he said softly.

I nodded. "Feels like it."

He looked at me with tired eyes. "Be careful now. After fire, things change."

He was right. The explosion wasn't just an accident. It was a turning point — for the refinery, for the island, for all of us working atop a powder keg pretending to be a workplace. And none of us knew it yet, but the hardest days were still ahead.

Aftershocks

The morning after the refinery blast, the island felt wrong. Not dangerous in the usual way — not the everyday risk you lived with — but *unbalanced*, like the whole place had been knocked sideways and was still deciding how to stand up again.

When I stepped outside, the air carried a chemical tang that hit the back of your throat. The wind had shifted overnight, pushing the smoke across the camps. Men walked around with cloths over their faces, eyes squinting. The sun was barely up and already the heat pressed down hard, trapping the smell close to the ground.

John was waiting by the pickup.

"Tool pusher wants everyone at the rig early," he said. "Says we need to check every line after what happened."

He didn't need to explain why. If the blast had shaken anything loose — even something small — it could spiral into disaster fast.

We drove toward the rig. The road was covered in a thin layer of dust and black grit. The blast wave must've carried it across the island. From the cab, the refinery still smoldered in the distance, sending up dark streaks of smoke. Even half a mile away, you could see burnt metal twisted like melted wire.

When we reached the site, the Iranian crew was already there. They looked exhausted. Dark patches under their eyes, movements stiff. A few had bandages around their wrists or arms from helping at the refinery. No complaints. No conversation about it. They just worked.

Hamid handed me a pair of gloves, the fabric still damp from being washed.

"Many lines loose," he said. "We must check all. Slowly."

Slow wasn't a luxury we usually had. But today it mattered.

We started with the choke manifold — the heart of the rig's defence when pressure kicked off. It was still intact, but some of the supports looked slightly shifted. You wouldn't notice unless you'd stared at them every day for months. But we had.

"Blast wave," John muttered. "Travelled through the ground."

He wasn't wrong. Steel doesn't lie.

We tightened bolts, realigned valves, and listened for tiny leaks. On a normal day, we worked fast. After a refinery explosion, you move like a surgeon. No hurry, no shortcuts. The island had shown us exactly what could happen if even one weak link gave way.

The Germans turned up half an hour later, faces pale, clothes too clean for what we were dealing with. Karl was gone now, replaced by another supervisor who introduced himself as Dieter. Same accent, same arrogance, but younger. He climbed up onto the platform and asked if the rig integrity had been "compromised."

I pointed at a crooked support we'd just corrected.

"There. That moved."

He frowned. "By how much?"

"A few millimetres."

He shrugged. "Is that significant?"

John stared at him. "If it wasn't, we'd be having coffee instead of tightening bolts."

Dieter made notes on a tablet and wandered off, probably writing something useless about compliance.

The day dragged. Heat built early and sat heavy around the rig. Sweat soaked through shirts. Sand from the blast grit stung every scrape on your hands. We crawled over the derrick, checked the pumps, traced every joint in the mud system. The explosion had sent a shock through the entire island — pipes, tanks, rigs, all of it — like a giant hitting the ground with a closed fist.

By late afternoon, we were running on fumes. The Iranian lads were drinking water straight from cylinders, not even bothering with cups. You could see how tired they were — shoulders sagging, hands trembling slightly when they set down tools.

During a break, I sat in the shade of the shale shaker house, legs stretched out. Hamid joined me, wiping dust from his eyes.

"Refinery still burning," he said.

"Will it hold?"

He shrugged. "Maybe. Maybe not."

There was no false comfort on Karg. Men didn't say things would be fine when they knew better.

As we rested, a deep boom rolled across the island — distant but unmistakable. We snapped our heads up. For a moment everything froze. Then another man shouted from the far side of the rig:

"Not explosion! They are depressuring tank!"

Hamid exhaled slowly.

"Island bleeding gas," he said. "They must release pressure."

And just like that, the work continued. Because when the island belched or groaned, you didn't panic. You just paid attention.

By the time we finished the checks, the sun was low, painting everything gold and dusty. The rig stood there like a battered monument — still crooked, still ugly, still alive. But now we trusted it again. Or as much as you could trust anything on Karg Island.

We drove back to camp in silence, both too tired to talk. Smoke still drifted across the sky. The refinery flare was burning weakly, as if struggling to stay lit.

As I stepped out of the Hilux, I realised something simple and frightening:

The explosion hadn't been the event.

It had been the warning.

And whatever came next, we weren't ready for it.

Pressure Lines

For days after the refinery blast, the island felt like it was holding its breath. You could sense it in the air, in the ground, in the way the men moved. Everyone waited for something else to go wrong. Nobody said it aloud, but we all knew it. Karg Island never gave you just one problem. It came in chains.

By midweek, the refinery crews had brought the fire under control, though "under control" was a flexible phrase on Karg. Flames still flickered from busted lines. Smoke curled up in steady ropes that hung over the island like a warning flag. From the rig floor you could see the glow at night, pulsing like a heartbeat.

We pushed on with drilling. The well didn't care that the refinery had almost blown itself off the map. Pressure kept climbing as we went deeper — not dramatically, but enough that you paid attention. Enough to make your shoulders tense when the pumps shifted tone.

The Iranian toolpusher, Farzad, didn't smile once that entire week. He walked around with a clipboard that looked like it had survived a war. His thumb traced the edges of every column of numbers like he was waiting for one to betray him.

"You feel it?" he asked me on the drill floor one night.

"What?"

He tapped the steel beneath our boots. "Island nervous."

That was the closest thing to poetry I ever heard from Farzad. But he was right. The ground carried tension. A kind of vibration you didn't hear — you sensed it.

The Germans, now led by Dieter, were trying to regain control of the operation with checklists and theoretical models. They gathered the Iranian supervisors for "briefings" about emergency response, as if the locals hadn't lived through decades of war, bombing, and industrial failures. You could see the frustration in the Iranians' faces. They listened politely, nodded, then went back to doing things the way that actually kept us alive.

Meanwhile, the company — this time under the banner of KCA-Deutag — sent out a string of emails telling us to "maintain operational continuity despite the incident." Easy words from an office far from the Gulf. None of them had tasted burning crude in the air.

One afternoon, Reza the mud engineer came into the doghouse with a look that made John sit up straight.

"Weight not stable," Reza said. "We add, still dropping."

John frowned. "Where's it going?"

Reza pointed down. "Formation taking it."

Lost circulation. Not the worst thing that could happen — unless it got away from you. Then you were balancing between a kick and a stuck pipe, like juggling knives blindfolded.

We slowed the pumps. Checked returns. Adjusted viscosity. Hours passed while we tried to coax the well back into something cooperative. Sweat ran down my back, soaking the waist of my overalls. The heat was constant, the smoke smell still hanging from the refinery like a curtain.

By dusk, we'd stabilised it — barely. The mud pits were lower than anyone liked, and we knew we'd be fiddling with the recipe for days. But the well was still ours. For now.

That night, as I walked back toward the camp, the island gave another long groan — a low, rolling echo that rumoured its way across the ground. I stopped. Ahead of me, the refinery flare flickered then flared up high before dropping again into a smaller flame.

John caught up to me.

"You hear that?"

"Hard to miss," I said.

"That wasn't a blast."

"No."

"Pressure dump?"

"Maybe. Or just the place shifting."

We stood there for a moment, watching the flare struggle, spitting small sparks into the dark like a faulty torch. The air felt heavy — not hot heavy, but weighted.

Back in camp, the Iranian lads ate in silence. Even the usual murmurs of conversation were gone. The only sound was the scrape of cutlery on metal plates.

Hamid sat beside me and nudged my arm.

"You go refinery today?"

"No."

He nodded. "Many problems. Pipes not good."

"From the explosion?"

He shook his head. "From before. Explosion just show it."

That stuck with me. Because it was true of everything on Karg — the blast wasn't the cause. It was the reveal. The island showed you the truth when it wanted to, not before.

Later that night, I walked down toward the shoreline. The sea was calm — a rare sight — the dark water lapping softly against the rocks. Across the Gulf, distant lights flickered from offshore platforms. A tanker moved slowly, engines a faint hum.

But the peace didn't sit right. It felt borrowed.

Behind me, the refinery gave another rumble, like a long exhale. The ground trembled for half a second. Then nothing. Silence.

I headed back to camp. As I reached the accommodation block, John stepped out of his room.

"Trouble?" he asked.

"Not yet," I said. "But it's coming."

He didn't disagree. He just ran a hand through his hair and muttered, "Figures."

The island wasn't finished with us. None of us said it, but we all felt it. Pressure was building — not just in the well, but in the metal, the soil, the men. Everything wound tight, waiting for the next shift in fate. And on Karg, when things shifted, they didn't do it quietly.

The Long Night

The final days of that rotation felt like living inside a coiled spring. The refinery was still limping, the well was misbehaving, and the whole island seemed to shift under us like an old ship straining at its bolts. Even the wind carried tension. Sharp, restless, full of grit that stuck to your teeth.

On the third night after the blast, I woke to a noise I couldn't place at first — not the usual hum of generators or distant machinery. This was deeper. A long, drawn-out thud that rolled through the air like something heavy falling somewhere far away. Not close enough to panic, not far enough to ignore.

I stepped outside. The sky was dark except for the refinery glow pulsing at the horizon. John was already standing there, hands on hips, staring toward it.

"You heard that too?" I asked.

"Yeah," he said. "Hoping it's just a tank settling."

"Tank settling doesn't sound like that."

He grunted. "Nothing on this island sounds the way it should."

We stood there listening for another sound, but the night settled again into uneasy quiet. A few Iranian workers walked past, heading toward the prayer building. Their faces were tired but calm — the kind of calm that only comes from seeing worse.

I followed John back inside, but sleep didn't come. Every creak of the accommodation frame made my eyes open again. The island felt alive, twitching under us.

By morning, the air was thick with smoke again. I could taste metal on my tongue. As I walked to the rig, the sun came up behind the refinery, turning the smoke into orange streaks. It was like the place was burning from the inside out.

Farzad met us at the rig, expression flat.

"Pressure building again," he said. "Slow, but building."

He handed John a sheet of numbers — hand-written, smudged. No printed reports out here. The blast had damaged half their systems.

As the day warmed up, the tension grew with the heat. The mud weight kept drifting. Not fast, but enough to keep the alarms twitching. Equipment we'd checked two days earlier now showed small leaks. Nothing disastrous yet — just the kind of problems that knew how to add up if you weren't watching.

Around mid-afternoon, the wind suddenly died. Just... stopped. The rig went eerily quiet. Even the sea sounded muffled. Hamid froze mid-step and looked up.

"Bad," he said softly. "Very bad."

A few seconds later, a vibration rolled through the drill floor. Not strong — more like a shiver. The steel under our boots hummed.

Reza ran from the mud pits. "Levels moving!" he yelled.

John leaned over the gauges. The mud line was creeping again. Not a kick, not yet. But pressure was shifting in a way none of us liked. We slowed the pumps, adjusted the weight, and watched the system like hawks.

Then, far off toward the refinery, came another dull boom — low, distant. The ground twitched again.

"Another tank?" I asked.

Farzad shook his head. "More pipes."

It was all he said, but the look in his eyes said the rest: the refinery wasn't steady, not even close.

The work dragged on for hours. Every adjustment on the well felt like trying to balance a tower of bricks on a shaking table. The Germans arrived again to "monitor," Dieter holding his tablet like it could save him. He asked if we'd filled out the new hazard forms.

John didn't even look at him. "No one gives a toss about forms right now."

Dieter opened his mouth, closed it again, and backed off. Maybe the island had finally gotten to him too. By the time the sun set, the smoke in the sky had turned crimson. The flare from the refinery burned brighter than usual, flickering like a signal. Men coughed as they walked, the air thick and bitter.

When the shift ended, I could barely lift my arms. The heat, the gas, the tension — it all sat heavy on my chest. I walked down toward the shoreline out of habit. Needed air that didn't smell like combustion. Needed to feel something steady. But even the sea didn't seem calm. Waves slapped harder than normal. The horizon was smeared with haze. Tanker lights flickered in the distance like half-dead fireflies.

Hamid found me sitting on a rock. He lowered himself beside me with a sigh that sounded older than he was.

"You think island finish?" he asked.

"No," I said. "Not yet."

He nodded slowly. "Then more trouble soon."

Neither of us spoke after that. We just sat there, staring out at the dark water, each lost in our own thoughts. The refinery flickered behind us like a dying lantern. Every so often you could hear another distant groan of metal.

Later, back in my room, I lay on the mattress staring at the ceiling. My ears rang with phantom alarms. My hands still shook from the day's strain. Outside, the island creaked and hissed like something alive. And as sleep finally dragged me under, one thought pressed hard and clear:

Karg wasn't done with us. Not by a long shot.

Chapter 9
The Well That Wouldn't Obey

When the Ground Started Talking Back

The morning the well turned on us didn't start with alarms or shouting. It started quietly — too quietly. The kind of hush that makes you check over your shoulder even when no one's there.

I stepped out of the accommodation block just as the sun was dragging itself over the horizon. The sky looked dirty, stained by smoke drifting from the refinery. Overnight, more piping had failed, according to the rumours filtering through camp. Nothing dramatic, nothing like the big blast — just leaks, flames, pressure dumps. "Minor events," the company called them. Minor events that shook the island.

I walked toward the rig with John, boots crunching over the gritty ground. The heat was already rising, pushing yesterday's smoke into a haze that hung low and sharp.

"You sleep?" he asked.

"Not really."

"Me neither. Island's got nerves."

That was the thing about Karg — it made grown men talk like superstitious sailors. But you couldn't blame them. Everything here felt alive. The refinery breathed, the well groaned, the earth hummed. You learned to listen the way you listen to a storm rolling in.

When we reached the rig, the Iranian crew was already gathered. Farzad, the toolpusher, held a clipboard but wasn't looking at it. His eyes were fixed on the derrick like he expected it to start moving by itself.

"What's wrong?" I asked.

He pointed to the drill line. "Listen."

I listened. At first, I heard nothing unusual — the low whir of generators, the clank of chains, the distant rumble from the refinery. But then I caught it: a faint, rhythmic vibration running up the steel. Too steady, too deliberate to be noise.

Reza walked over from the mud tanks, wiping his hands on a rag. He didn't speak. Just shook his head slowly.

John leaned in. "Torque spike?"

"Not yet," Reza said. "Soon."

That was worse than a yes.

We started the shift cautious. Pumps low, weight steady, watching every gauge like it might jump. The mud pits shimmered under the sun, the surface trembling slightly with each circulation pulse. A bad sign. Mud should behave. When it starts fidgeting, something's pushing back.

Farzad sent two men to check the choke manifold. I followed them. The steel walkway burned through my gloves as

123

I steadied myself. The aftershocks from the refinery had shifted half the rig's alignment, and although we'd fixed the obvious issues, there was no telling what hairline cracks we hadn't found.

The manifold was warm — too warm. The gas lines nearby hummed with a low vibration that felt like a warning. One of the Iranian lads, tiny but sharp-eyed, crouched beside a flange and pressed his fingers to it. He pulled back immediately.

"Hot," he said. "Not good."

That was enough for me. We climbed back to the drill floor.

Reza approached with a sample tin. The mud inside was darker than it should've been. Thicker too.

"Cuttings changing," he said. "Formation different now."

John took the tin, sniffed it, and swore. "We're entering the bastard zone."

The logs had hinted at a nasty pressure pocket below — the kind that didn't care if you were ready or not. With the refinery still unstable and the island groaning like an old hull in heavy seas, this was the last thing we needed.

Then the first spike hit.

The standpipe pressure jumped — not a huge leap, but sharp. Enough to snap heads around. Alarms stayed silent, but the movement was too quick to ignore.

Farzad stepped forward. "Slow pumps. Add weight."

We did as he said. The well didn't calm. Another spike. Higher this time.

Reza muttered something in Farsi, voice low and tense.

John glanced at me. "We're dancing with it now."

Pressure kept building in tiny increments, like the well was testing us. The mud pump rhythm went uneven. Not violently — just slightly off-beat. But that tiny shift was all it took to raise every hair on your neck.

Hamid walked over with masks in his hands. He didn't give an explanation. He didn't need to. If Hamid thought you might need a mask, you took the bloody mask.

We strapped them to our belts.

The drill line started to tremble harder — not violently, but enough that Farzad raised a hand to silence everyone.

"Stop," he said. "Listen."

We did. The rig floor hummed, a deep bass vibration rising through the metal grating.

Reza looked at me. "Pressure coming from down, not pump."

"Formation pushing back?"

He nodded once.

And then —

THUMP.

A solid, heavy jolt reverberated through the entire structure. Not a kick. Not a collapse. Something else — something shifting. The gauges fluttered. Mud surged slightly in the flowline. Reza and Farzad shouted instructions at the same time, voices overlapping, both of them moving fast.

We responded on instinct. Slowed circulation, adjusted weight, eased off tension. The whole rig groaned like a crane under too much load. The rumbling continued — long, steady, deep. Like the earth clearing its throat.

John leaned close. "This isn't just the well."

"What then?"

He shook his head. "Don't know. But the island's talking."

Another vibration rolled through the ground, heavier this time, almost like footsteps. You could feel it in your ribs.

Farzad stared toward the refinery, jaw clenched. Smoke drifted sideways across the horizon like torn cloth.

"This is beginning," he said quietly. "Not end."

And for the first time since I'd arrived on Karg, I believed him.

The First Kick

Once the ground started that slow, unsettling vibration, the whole rig tightened up like a clenched fist. Nobody spoke unless they had to. Even the Germans kept quiet, which was a miracle in itself. The air felt heavy, like it was waiting for something to drop.

Reza checked the mud properties again and came back shaking his head.

"Weight good. Gel good. But pressure..."

He made a flat-handed motion rising upward.

John frowned. "Formation pressure shouldn't be this high yet."

"Shouldn't be," Reza said. "But is."

We'd seen the logs. We knew the zone below us was tricky, but not *this* tricky. The island had shifted after the refinery blast — maybe underground pressures redistributed, maybe faults moved, maybe something deeper had cracked. Whatever it was, the well didn't care about paperwork or projections. It wanted to push back.

Hamid grabbed the choke manifold keys without being told. That's when I knew things were serious. He only did that when he expected trouble.

The pumps were still running soft when the next sign hit — the flowline twitched. Not violently, but enough to make Farzad's head snap toward it.

"Stop!" he shouted.

We froze. Everyone stared at the flow. A thin tremble rippled through the mud. That was pressure talking.

Farzad leaned over the gauges, his jaw grinding. "Stand by... stand by..."

The standpipe needle crept upward another hair.

Then another.

Then two more, faster.

"Kick," Reza said. "Small one, but yes."

Farzad didn't waste time. "Choke ready!"

Hamid spun the valves, muscle memory taking over. He didn't look scared — he looked focused, the way a man looks when he's fought this battle before and survived but never forgotten the cost.

John eased off the pumps. The mud level in the pits dropped a fraction too fast.

"Gas cutting the returns," he muttered. "Bugger's pushing."

"Hold steady," Farzad warned. "Hold..."

Then the well coughed.

There's no other way to describe it. A sudden thump through the drill string, a shudder through the derrick, followed by a surge of mud spitting up the flowline like a slapped dog.

The alarm stayed silent — not malfunctioning, just lagging behind reality. Real kicks don't wait for machinery.

Hamid cracked the choke a notch. The hiss of pressure bleeding off sang through the rig, sharp and mean. Mud shot out, darker now, flecked with fine cutting. Gas bubbled through the returns.

"Easy!" Farzad barked. "Not too fast!"

If you bleed a kick too quickly, you risk sucking formation fluids up faster — a chain reaction you never want. If you go too slow, pressure builds and the well climbs into your lap. There's no manual for the perfect middle ground. It's feel. Experience. Nerve.

The Germans hovered uselessly behind us. Dieter finally spoke.

"Should we not shut in completely?"

Farzad rounded on him. "You shut in at wrong time, you blow whole rig."

Dieter went pale and shut his mouth.

I glanced at Reza. He was watching the mud like it was alive. "Gas. Not oil," he murmured. "Light gas. Dangerous."

He wasn't exaggerating. The wrong spark, a static charge, or a stray tool strike and we'd be scattered across the Gulf.

The pressure needle trembled again, then climbed another notch. Not a big jump — a sly one. The kind that made your skin go cold.

John muttered, "It's building underneath us. Wants out."

The whole structure groaned. The same deep vibration from earlier returned, stronger this time. Not just the well — the entire island felt like it was turning over in its sleep.

Hamid adjusted the choke again. Mud gurgled through the line. A thin mist sprayed up where it shouldn't have, sparkling in the sunlight. Gas-laden mist. We all stepped back instinctively.

Then the refinery rumbled in the distance — another pressure dump, or another small explosion. Hard to tell. The sound crawled across the ground, a low tremor that made the rig shudder.

The well surged again.

This time the spike hit fast. The standpipe needle jumped several bars in one go.

Alarms screamed.

Mud splashed up violently.

Reza yelled something in Farsi — urgent, sharp.

Farzad slammed his hand down:

"SHUT IT!"

Hamid spun the choke hard, snapping it into control mode. John cut the pumps. The drill string clanged with released tension. Gas hissed through the system like a wild animal behind a cage door.

Everything vibrated — the derrick, the floor, even the handrails under my grip.

Farzad counted under his breath, watching the numbers like a gambler waiting on the last card.

"Hold... hold... HOLD—"

The needle slowed.

Then steadied.

Then began to drop, fraction by fraction.

Hamid exhaled like he'd been holding his breath for an hour.

Reza wiped sweat from his face. "That was not small kick," he said quietly.

"No," John said. "That was the well saying hello."

We stood there in silence, listening to the equipment hiss and settle, the alarms winding down, the mud tanks burping gas.

Farzad turned to us, face grim.

"Today we were lucky. Tomorrow maybe not."

He wasn't trying to scare us.

He was telling the truth the way Karg Island told it — plain, heavy, without room for argument. And none of us disagreed.

The Second Push

You'd think after a kick like that, the well would settle for a bit. It didn't. If anything, it felt like we'd poked something awake. The pressure simmered under us — not enough to trigger alarms, but enough that everyone walked with their shoulders lifted, listening for the faintest shift.

The next morning, the air tasted like burnt carbon. Overnight, another flare line at the refinery had ruptured. No big explosion, but enough of a flame burst that half the island saw the flash. The Iranians took it in stride. Another day, another problem. But the refinery incident had rattled the well in ways the company didn't understand from their desks in Dubai.

John and I reached the rig before sunrise. Farzad was already on the drill floor, staring at the gauges like they owed him an answer.

"Pressure stable?" I asked.

He gave a slow shrug. "Stable for now. But pressure below…"

He tapped the steel grating with his boot. "Unhappy."

That was Farzad's gift — he didn't dramatise. He just stated facts the way a man states the weather.

Reza approached with another mud sample, this one lighter, almost foamy at the top.

"Gas cut," he said. "Same as yesterday."

John groaned. "Bastard's still breathing at us."

We started the shift gentle — low pumps, steady rotation, careful weight. The Iranian floorhands moved with that reserved precision they had when danger hovered close. Even Dieter, the young German supervisor, kept his distance from the active lines. For once, he seemed to understand that paperwork couldn't save him.

By mid-morning, the hum returned — that same deep vibration rising through the metal, like the island clearing its throat again.

Hamid looked up at the derrick. "Not good," he murmured. "Not good at all."

The well began pushing. Not hard, not fast — but consistently. The standpipe needle crept upward by fractions. Reza frowned at the mud returns.

"More gas," he said. "More than yesterday."

And then it hit.

Not a jump — a **lift**.

The drill string shuddered upward a half-inch like something beneath had flicked it with a finger.

Farzad reacted instantly. "Slow! Don't fight it!"

John eased back on rotation. The whole rig floor vibrated with a hollow metallic thrum.

Then the mud level rose — slow at first, then quicker. Thick, gas-whipped, unstable.

I shouted, "Kick coming!"

Farzad raised his hand. "Standby choke!"

Hamid was already there, hands on the valves, jaw clenched. You could see the calculation in Farzad's eyes — how fast to bleed, how much to hold, how long before gas broke through somewhere it shouldn't.

The spike hit a heartbeat later.

The standpipe pressure jumped.

The alarms screamed.

Mud splattered up the flowline like a struck artery.

"CHOKE!" Farzad roared.

Hamid cracked the valve. Gas hissed through the line like a steam train. The well heaved — a deep, angry surge that rattled the derrick. The drill crew braced themselves.

The air filled with the stink of sour gas — faint but unmistakable. Not H_2S levels yet, but enough to raise the hairs on your arms.

Reza pointed at the mud pit. "Cutting heavy now! Very heavy!"

John grimaced. "Formation's collapsing or shifting."

The gauges danced. Not wildly — but snappy enough to mean the well was fighting back, uncertain whether to push harder or settle.

Dieter panicked.

"Shut everything! Shut all valves!"

Farzad snapped at him. "You shut wrong valve, we die!"

Dieter backed away, hands up, face drained white.

Hamid kept the choke precisely between danger and control, fingers turning millimetres at a time. A man who'd done this often enough to understand the difference between bleeding pressure and inviting disaster.

The vibration under our boots built again.

A long, steady tremor rolled through the structure.

"I don't like that," John muttered.

"Not well," Reza said. "Island."

He was right. The ground felt alive.

Then — **THUMP**.

A deeper jolt than the day before. The derrick groaned. Bolts squeaked. Something far below us shifted, like a giant rolling in its sleep.

The pressure needle jerked up one last time.

Farzad shouted, "HOLD THE LINE!"

Hamid fought the choke. The hiss turned to a roar. Mud fountained into the return trough, thick with gas, bubbling like a furious pot about to boil over.

For a moment — too long a moment — the pressure didn't respond. It held, stubborn, defiant. Every man on the drill floor stopped breathing.

Then the needle...

Slowed.

Wavered.

Dropped — half a bar, then a full bar.

Hamid exhaled. "Good," he whispered.

The well grumbled like something displeased, but it settled. Mud stopped boiling. The alarms quieted. Gas bled away in a long hiss until only the island's distant groans remained.

Farzad looked at us — sweat streaked, jaw tight.

"That was second warning," he said. "Next time, maybe not warning."

He wasn't wrong.

We all felt it.

The well wasn't finished.

It was choosing when to strike.

The Breaking Edge

The night after the second kick was the longest night I'd had on Karg yet, and that's saying something. The island didn't sleep. You could hear distant rumbles from the refinery — pressure dumps, metal groaning, the odd flare cough that echoed off the rocks. Every sound carried a hint of threat.

Inside my room, the walls creaked like the building was made of old ship timber instead of steel. The air was thick, hot, sour with refinery smoke. When the generators dipped for a moment and the lights flickered, I sat up straight, heart hammering, half expecting the whole island to lurch.

By morning, I felt like I hadn't slept at all.

The walk to the rig was different this time. Men weren't talking. The usual muttering and swearing had dried up. The Iranian crew walked with their heads slightly down, like they were listening for something under their feet. Even John stayed quiet, jaw tight as he scanned the horizon.

"Anything from the refinery?" I asked.

He shook his head. "Official line is everything's stable."

We both snorted. "Stable" on Karg meant nothing.

When we reached the rig, Farzad was waiting, hands on hips. His expression said enough — things were worse.

"See this," he said, pointing at the gauge panel.

The standpipe pressure was fluctuating — tiny movements, but constant. A living pulse. You didn't want that. A well should behave until you force it to move. This one was shifting on its own.

Reza came over holding a fresh sample tin. The mud inside was flecked with finer cuttings than before — not normal for the depth we were at.

"Formation breaking," he said quietly. "Not full collapse. But close."

John rubbed his face. "Last thing we need."

Farzad nodded. "We hold it. Carefully."

We eased the pumps up, watching every number like it might explode. The first hour passed without incident, though the drill string vibrated more than usual. A faint clatter echoed through the derrick. The kind of noise you remember years later.

Hamid walked over with masks again, handing them out without a word. He didn't meet anyone's eyes.

"Expecting gas?" I asked him.

He shook his head. "Expecting... something."

Not reassuring.

The second hour was worse. The mud pits frothed slightly at the surface — gas still creeping through. Not enough to trigger alarms, but enough to make you nervous. The flowline twitched every few minutes, like the well was adjusting its shoulders.

Dieter appeared with his tablet, pointing at the graphs like they meant anything.

"This fluctuation is outside standard—"

Farzad cut him off. "Standard is for safe rigs. This is not safe rig."

Dieter hesitated, then stepped back. Even he could sense the tension.

Around midday, the refinery groaned again — a long, low moan rolling across the island. The ground trembled. Tools rattled on shelves. Everyone looked toward the horizon, expecting smoke. None came.

"Pressure dump," John said. "Big one."

Farzad's eyes narrowed. "Dump changes underground pressure."

We all knew what that meant.

We got the proof ten minutes later.

The drill line jerked — not up, not down, but sideways. A strange movement. Wrong. The sort of thing you only feel once before your instincts start yelling.

Reza shouted from the mud tanks. "Pressure dropping fast!"

John ran to the gauges. "We're losing returns!"

A lost-circulation event at that depth was bad. But paired with the refinery's instability and the well's recent mood, it was something else entirely — a sign the formation beneath us was shifting.

Farzad pointed at the choke manifold. "Be ready!"

Hamid moved like lightning, hands hovering over the valves.

The pressure drop continued — ten bars, then fifteen.

"Jesus," John muttered. "Where's it going?"

Reza answered without looking up. "Everywhere. Formation taking everything."

The well suddenly felt empty — hollow. A dangerous feeling. An empty well-meant unpredictable behaviour. Gas could surge up fast. Pressure could flip. The whole system turned unstable.

Then the standpipe needle lurched upward — violently this time.

"Kick again!" Farzad roared.

Hamid snapped the choke open. Gas shrieked through the line. Mud burped up the flowline like something alive was pushing behind it.

The derrick shook. Tools clattered off racks. A hard metallic scream tore through the drill string.

Reza pointed at a rising plume in the mud trough. "Gas! Heavy gas!"

John gritted his teeth. "Big one this time."

Hamid fought the choke like he was wrestling a live wire. His arms strained, sweat pouring down his face. The pressure needle jittered wildly.

Then the island groaned — a long, deep sound that rolled through the ground and up the legs of the rig.

For a moment, everything felt weightless.

The well surged again — harder than before. The rig floor jolted. Mud splashed across the steel like a wave. Alarms blared in every direction.

"SHUT IT! SHUT IT NOW!" Farzad screamed.

Hamid locked the choke tight. John cut the pumps. The entire system shuddered, then held — barely.

The pressure climbed...

Climbed...

Hung there like a held breath...

Then slowly, painfully, crawled downward.

No one spoke.

When the numbers finally steadied, Farzad exhaled through his nose and said:

"That was not warning. That was promise."

He didn't need to explain what he meant.

The well wasn't misbehaving anymore.

It was threatening.

And deep down, all of us knew — the next time it pushed, we might not be fast enough.

Chapter 10
The Island Closes its Fist

The Day the Sky Went Wrong

The morning the island finally tipped over into madness started hotter than usual. Even before dawn, the heat felt wrong — thick, unmoving, like the whole place was holding in a breath. The refinery glow was still burning on the horizon, a dull angry orange behind the smoke. Nobody said anything as we walked toward the rig. No banter. No complaints. Just heavy footsteps and heavier faces.

John lit a cigarette, took one drag, then flicked it away. "Too bloody still," he muttered.

He was right. The air wasn't moving. Even the sea sounded muffled. Karg felt like it had shut its doors.

The Iranian lads were already gathered on the drill floor when we arrived. Farzad was standing with his arms folded, staring out toward the refinery like he could see something the rest of us couldn't.

"What's the story?" I asked him.

He didn't look away from the horizon. "Trouble," he said simply.

We waited, watching the glow in the distance. Then a low rumble rolled across the island — slow, deep, like thunder under the ground. You felt it in your knees first, then your ribs. Tools on the racks rattled. A bolt clinked its way off a shelf and hit the floor.

Reza jogged up from the mud tanks, breathing hard. "Lines again," he said. "Refinery... something break."

That was an understatement. The ground shivered lightly beneath us, like the whole island was shifting on its own axis.

John squinted into the haze. "That's not a flare. That's bigger."

He was right. A glow pulsed behind the refinery structures, not a steady burn — a rising-and-dropping kind of light, the sort you only see when something's gone wrong with pressure.

For a solid minute, nobody spoke.

Then came the sound.

Not a boom — a **snap**.

Sharp. Metallic. Violent.

It cracked through the morning air like a giant metal rope breaking loose.

Then the flare stack belched a jet of black smoke that mushroomed up fast. A second later, a deeper roar followed — the unmistakable sound of a pressure line rupturing.

"Christ," John whispered. "That's a bad one."

Farzad finally turned toward us. "We finish quick today," he said. "Maybe no shift tonight."

Hamid snorted. "If island still here tonight."

He meant it as a joke, but nobody laughed.

The sun dragged itself up over the water, casting long shadows across the desert rock. The smoke drifted sideways now, blown by a sudden gust. That wind came out of nowhere — a hard, hot slap that carried the stink of burning crude.

We started the shift, though everyone moved like they were expecting the ground to open up beneath them. The well had been unpredictable for days, and after two near-blowouts, nobody trusted it. The mud pits looked uneasy again — ripples across the surface like small fingers tapping.

Reza didn't like it. "Gas again," he muttered. "Always gas now."

John sighed. "Place is falling apart."

Half an hour in, the horizon flickered.

A bright flash — white, then gold — lit the refinery silhouette.

Then came the boom.

Not as big as the first explosion days ago, but enough to make the rig shudder. Dust drifted off the handrails. A ladder creaked, metal straining.

I grabbed the rail to steady myself. "Another one gone?"

Farzad nodded grimly. "Second flare line. More pressure in system. More chance boom again."

The Iranians moved with tight, efficient steps. They weren't panicking — they'd lived through worse — but they weren't wasting time either.

The company, of course, sent a message through the radio:

"Operations remain stable. Continue work."

John laughed without humour. "Stable my arse."

As the morning dragged on, the sounds from the refinery got stranger — hollow bangs, rattling echoes, short bursts like metal coughing. Every noise made the crew flinch.

At one point, a vibration rolled through the drill floor, subtle but steady. The drill string hummed with a strange resonance. You could feel it through your boots.

Reza glanced at me. "Pressure underground move again."

"Connected to the refinery?" I asked.

"Yes," he said. "Everything connected on island. You break one thing, all things change."

By midday, the smoke plume had widened, thick as wool, drifting low across the desert. The sun disappeared behind it, turning everything an ugly brown-yellow. You couldn't see the refinery clearly anymore — just the occasional flash between the haze. Then word spread — badly translated, passed from worker to worker:

The rig offshore had been hit.

Not our rig — the drilling platform a few miles away. Something had struck it. Explosion. Some said sabotage. Some said stray ordnance. No one knew. No one trusted the official line. But the important bit was simple:

A rig had gone down.

That news cut through the crew like a knife.

John's face went slack. "If they're hitting rigs now..."

He didn't finish. He didn't need to.

Farzad walked over, eyes dark. "Finish tasks. Then go camp. Quickly."

"Are we shutting down?" I asked.

He paused. "Not yet."

Then quietly: "But soon."

The wind picked up again, carrying the smell of burning crude right through the rig floor. The island groaned once more — long, low, unsettling.

Something was shifting.

Something fundamental.

This wasn't just a bad well anymore.

Or a bad refinery.

Or a bad week.

Karg Island was failing. Breaking apart under its own pressure.

And we were standing right on top of it.

When the Boats Stopped Smiling

After the second refinery rupture, the atmosphere around the island changed completely. You could feel it most at the jetty — the place that was supposed to be the "safe point," the link to Kharg Island and the mainland. But that morning, even the boats looked nervous. The crews stood quieter, glancing at the horizon like something might rise out of it.

John and I were heading down to check on supplies when we noticed the Saudi crew clustered together near the ramp. They weren't normally the chatty type, but today they were whispering with their shoulders tight.

"What's that about?" John asked.

I shrugged. "Probably heard the rig offshore went down."

One of the Saudis caught my eye — a broad-shouldered lad with a faded baseball cap. He looked spooked. Really spooked. He lifted his hands in a helpless "what now?" gesture, then pointed toward the guard post near the waterline.

Two Iranian soldiers stood there with rifles across their chests, talking in low voices. They had always been around, but today they weren't just loitering. Today they were watching.

"More of them every day," John muttered.

It was true. Armed personnel had doubled in the last week. Officially, they were there to "maintain refinery security." Unofficially, nobody knew who they answered to.

The boat captain waved at us from the deck. His beard looked scruffier than usual, his eyes bloodshot.

"You going out today?" he asked.

"Just supplies," I said. "Quick in and out."

He shook his head. "Quick not exist today."

Before I could ask what he meant, the first warning shot cracked across the water.

A single pop — sharp, unmistakable.

Everyone froze.

Another shot followed. This one closer. The Saudis flinched and ducked behind a stack of crates. The Iranian guards shouted something we didn't catch.

John's voice dropped. "What the hell?"

The boat captain held out his hand like a traffic officer. "Stay down. Stay quiet."

More shouting from the shoreline. Quick, angry Farsi. Then a burst of three shots — not aimed at us, but close enough to send echoes bouncing off the metal siding.

The Saudis huddled tighter. One of them kept repeating something under his breath — a prayer, I think. Their foreman stood rigid, eyes fixed on the guards.

Finally, one of the soldiers lifted a hand toward the Saudis, barked a few orders, and aimed his rifle into the air like a threat.

The Saudi foreman didn't move.

Then he turned — fast — and signalled his men back toward the camp.

The soldier lifted his rifle again.

The Saudi foreman hesitated... then stepped back anyway.

147

The guard fired another warning shot.

"That's enough," the captain hissed. "Back up the ramp. Slowly. Don't run."

We did as he said, moving one step at a time. The Saudis followed, keeping low, eyes wide. No one wanted to give the soldiers a reason to shoot properly.

When we reached the top of the jetty, John whispered, "You seeing what I'm seeing?"

"Yeah," I said. "No one's meant to leave today."

Back at camp, the rumours spread instantly:

"Saudis got shot at."

"They tried to board without clearance."

"Someone took a boat without permission."

"Someone's kid messed with a guard."

"They thought we were sabotaging something."

"Cover-up coming."

Every version contradicted the last. The only certain part was the gunfire.

Farzad gathered the drill crew near the tool shed. "No one go jetty unless I say," he told them. "Today very dangerous. Men with guns not calm."

Hamid nodded slowly. "Something happen last night. Something big."

No one knew what, but the refinery glow had been brighter than usual. A column of smoke had risen straight up for hours — too steady to be normal.

The company finally radioed a statement:

"Minor instability at refinery. All operations stable. Continue work."

The phrase "minor instability" had become a joke by then.

John rolled his eyes. "Minor my arse. They're shooting at crews now."

We returned to the rig after lunch, though "work" was the wrong word for what we were doing. It felt more like marking time while we waited for the next disaster. Every clang of metal made someone jump. Even Reza, calm as a monk most days, kept looking over his shoulder.

Hours passed. The sky got darker, clouded with smoke. The ground kept that faint vibration running underneath everything — not constant, but regular enough that nobody forgot it.

Then, around mid-afternoon, a runner from the refinery arrived. His face was grey with dust, his shirt half unbuttoned, his eyes wild.

He said one sentence in English:

"Rig... bomb... offshore... gone."

Then he repeated it in Farsi for Farzad.

The drill crew went dead silent.

John whispered, "Not ours?"

"Not ours," Farzad confirmed. "Other one. But very bad."

I felt cold despite the heat.

An offshore rig down meant this wasn't just industrial chaos anymore.

Something — or someone — was targeting assets.

John looked toward the sea. "If that had been us..."

He didn't need to finish.

The refinery groaned again — long, low, shuddering.

The island felt like it was closing in.

And for the first time since arriving, every man on that drill floor understood the same thing:

We needed to get off Karg. Soon.

The Captain Loses His Nerve

By the time afternoon settled into that sickly brown haze, everyone on Karg understood the situation: *We were trapped until someone in charge said otherwise.*

And no one knew who was actually in charge anymore.

The company said one thing.

The refinery crews said another.

The armed guards had their own rules.

And the island itself had a schedule none of us could read.

We finished the shift early — not because the work was done, but because Farzad insisted.

"Go camp," he told us. "No safe here now."

When a man like Farzad said something wasn't safe, you didn't argue.

We walked back toward the accommodation blocks, boots dragging through the grit, eyes stinging from the smoke drifting over the island. The light had gone strange — dim but sharp, like the sun was filtered through sandpaper.

At the camp gate, we saw movement down by the jetty. A group of men stood around one of the crew boats. The captain — a wiry Iranian in his fifties who normally carried himself like he owned the entire Gulf — was pacing up and down the deck, shouting at two soldiers.

John squinted. "What now?"

We walked closer. One of the Saudis waved us over with jittery hands.

"Captain crazy today," he said. "He want leave island."

The captain's voice carried across the water. He wasn't speaking English, but we didn't need a translation.

He was panicking.

The soldiers blocked the ramp, rifles held low but firm.

The captain jabbed a finger toward the horizon — toward the refinery, which was still belching smoke in waves — then toward the open sea.

"He wants to go," the Saudi said. "Says no one safe here."

John snorted. "He's not wrong."

Another flare shot up near the refinery — this one sharp and bright — followed by a metallic groan that rolled across the island. Everyone flinched.

The captain tried to push past the soldiers. One shoved him back. He stumbled, grabbed the rail, then lashed out with a string of curses. His crew tried to calm him, but he shook them off.

"He's done," John muttered. "He's had enough."

To be fair, so had everyone else.

The captain suddenly stopped shouting. He stood there breathing hard, chest rising and falling like a man who'd just sprinted a mile. Then he looked straight at us — really looked — and for the first time since I'd met him, I saw fear, plain and raw.

He pointed at the sea again, then at the refinery, then tapped his temple.

"Boom," he said in broken English. "More boom coming."

No one doubted it.

A refinery engineer walked up behind us, sweating through his shirt. "Captain tried to leave," he muttered. "They told him nobody leaves until inspection team arrives."

John rubbed his face. "Inspection team? From where?"

The engineer shrugged. "Tehran."

That was the worst answer possible. If a team was coming from the capital, it meant whatever had happened offshore wasn't a small thing. And they weren't going to let anyone leave before sorting the story.

We drifted back toward camp. Men whispered in half a dozen languages. The Saudis stuck together, eyes darting toward the guards. The Pakistani cooks had abandoned the kitchen and were standing outside, arms folded, listening for distant booms.

Through the smoke, you could see the silhouette of the refinery flare pulsing like a heartbeat. Every few minutes, another rattle or clank echoed across the island — pressure moving through pipes, metal expanding, maybe something worse.

Inside the accommodation block, the air was thick. The map on the wall rattled every time the ground gave one of those low, rolling vibrations.

Hamid came into the corridor carrying a small bag.

"You leaving?" I asked.

He shook his head. "No helo. No boat. I just... ready."

We nodded. Nobody judged him.

Around sunset, the captain appeared in camp, shoulders slumped. He'd been escorted by two guards, who hovered like angry shadows. His eyes were glassy, like he'd aged ten years in a day.

"What happened?" John asked.

"He no go," Hamid translated quietly. "Soldiers say: wait."

The captain muttered something under his breath. The only word I caught was "bomb."

We sat outside on the concrete steps, eating whatever passed for dinner — rice, oily chicken, something green no one could identify. Every clang in the distance made the whole group pause. Men ate fast, like they didn't want to be caught with a mouthful if something went wrong.

After a while, Farzad came over, wiping sweat from his brow.

"Listen," he said. "Tonight... maybe more trouble. Stay close to camp. No one wander. No jetty. No sea."

"What's happening?" I asked.

He hesitated, choosing the simplest English he had.

"Something wrong offshore. Something wrong refinery. Something wrong security. Nobody agree."

That summed it up perfectly.

As the sky darkened, the island grew louder. Odd pops from the refinery. Distant metallic bangs. The ocean slapped the rocks harder than usual, like the tide itself was restless.

Around 9pm, a flash lit the horizon — faint but unmistakable.

Not lightning.

Not a flare.

Something else.

The Saudis jumped to their feet.

John stood slowly.

Hamid sighed like a man who expected it.

Farzad didn't move. He just muttered, "This place finished."

And for the first time, the thought settled across all of us like a weight:

We might not get off this island alive.

The Last Boat Out

By dawn the next morning, the island felt beaten. Even the wind had stopped trying. A layer of smoke sat low over everything, thick enough that you could taste metal at the back of your throat. Men walked in silence, eyes half-open, bodies running on whatever scraps of sleep they'd managed the night before.

John and I made our way to the drill floor out of habit, not expectation. Nobody had said "shutdown," but everyone knew it was coming. You couldn't run a rig properly when the ground trembled every few hours and half the refinery behind you was coughing fire.

Farzad met us halfway.

"No drill today," he said. "Company say wait."

John raised an eyebrow. "Wait for what?"

Farzad just lifted one hand toward the haze behind the refinery. "For that to stop."

It wasn't going to.

We drifted back to camp with the others. The Saudis stayed close to the walls, glancing toward the shoreline where the armed guards still paced. Their foreman looked exhausted, like he'd aged five years since the shots yesterday.

Around mid-morning, a runner came from the security office — a skinny kid with dust in his beard and sweat cutting lines down his face. He shouted something in Farsi, and Hamid translated:

"Inspection cancelled. Jetty open. Boats move soon."

The words were like water poured on hot metal. Steam. Hisses. A kind of disbelief.

John blinked. "We're getting off?"

Hamid shrugged. "Maybe. If guards let us."

Men hurried to grab bags. There wasn't excitement so much as urgency — like a fire alarm had gone off and everyone was too tired to run but too scared to stay.

The boat captain was already at the jetty when we arrived, pacing the ramp like a man guarding treasure. He looked different from the day before — calmer, but with a hard edge in his eyes.

"You go quick," he said. "One trip. Maybe two. Not more."

"Why only two?" I asked.

He held up a finger. "Because island finish today."

No exaggeration in his voice. Just certainty.

As we walked down the jetty, an Iranian soldier stepped in front of us, blocking the way. His face was tight, his grip on the rifle a little too firm.

"Stop," he barked.

The captain strode up, shouting back at him. They argued in rapid Farsi, both gesturing at the sea, the horizon, the boat, the sky. The soldier shook his head at first. Then the captain jabbed a finger toward the refinery — which, as if on cue, groaned loudly, sending a deep vibration through the boards under our feet.

That settled it.

The soldier stepped aside.

We moved fast down the ramp and onto the boat. The deck bucked under our boots as men piled in: Saudis, Iranians, a few refinery hands who looked like they hadn't slept in days. The air smelled of diesel and fear.

John leaned close. "Keep your head low. If they change their minds, I don't fancy arguing."

The captain shouted something to his crew, and the boat's engines rumbled awake. The vibration felt good — like something dependable, something that wanted to move. The deckhands untied the ropes, and we pushed away from the jetty.

For a moment, the sea was still. Too still.

Then we gained speed.

As the island drifted further behind us, the refinery came into view through the smoke — a jagged silhouette, half-hidden, half-burning. Pipes that should've been straight were bent. A flare stack belched a dirty plume sideways, as if the whole structure had slumped.

No one spoke.

About halfway across the channel, John nudged me. "Look."

I turned.

At first I couldn't see what he meant — just the usual blur of heat and haze.

Then it happened.

A flash — bright and sharp — lit the outline of the offshore platform.

Not ours.

The other one.

A split second later, the sound reached us — a deep, booming thud that rolled across the water like a giant slamming a fist.

Then a second flash tore through the structure.

The rig folded in on itself — slow, like it was kneeling — before a column of black smoke shot up into the sky.

Someone on the boat gasped.

Someone else crossed themselves.

The Saudis huddled closer.

The captain said nothing. He only pushed the throttle harder.

John whispered, "If we'd been on nights..."

He didn't finish.

He didn't need to.

We sped through the channel in heavy silence, the boat slamming through waves, the island shrinking behind us. The heat, the smoke, the noise — all of it fell away bit by bit until only the open sea remained.

When we reached the mainland dock, nobody cheered. Nobody clapped. Men stepped off the boat like they were afraid the ground might disappear beneath them.

The captain leaned against the rail, staring back toward the island.

"It's finished," he said quietly. "Karg no good now."

He was right.

Whatever we'd left behind — the refinery, the well, the guards, the noise, the fear — it was gone, in the sense that it wasn't coming back.

John put a hand on my shoulder. "Come on," he said. "We're done here."

And just like that, without ceremony or farewell, we walked away — clothes stinking of smoke, nerves shot, grateful for the simple miracle of being alive.

Behind us, the horizon flickered again.

Karg Island wasn't just breaking.

It was collapsing.

And we'd escaped by hours, maybe minutes — a sliver of luck in a place that had nearly killed us.

Chapter 11
Cold Front

Russia

When the offer came, I didn't hesitate. I'd had enough of the chaos on the island, enough of watching things blow up around me. A steady job in **Russia** sounded almost civilised. The company had a decent reputation, the pay wasn't bad, and they wanted someone who could run nights without falling apart. That was me. Or at least I thought it was.

The flight dropped me in a city that looked frozen in time. Concrete blocks, grey skies, men with faces that didn't give much away. Nobody rushed. Nobody smiled either. It was the sort of cold that got into your teeth when you breathed in.

A driver met me with a sign. No conversation, just a nod and a walk to a battered 4x4 with tyres bald enough to make you pray. The roads were hard-packed snow, the sort that turned into sheet ice if the temperature shifted a degree. He never once touched the brake. Just downshifted and let the engine drag us to whatever speed he considered safe.

The camp was functional, nothing more. Prefab buildings lined up like they'd been dropped there by accident. Heat blasting at full tilt, windows dripping with condensation. The mess hall smelled of boiled cabbage and diesel. But compared to Iran, it felt like a holiday. Nobody shot at us. Nothing exploded in the night. The worst danger was slipping on the stairs after a snowstorm.

The rig itself was a different beast. Big, heavy, stubborn machinery that didn't like the cold any more than I did. Hydraulic lines froze solid, steel cracked if you looked at it wrong, and the men worked with scarves wrapped up to their eyes so their breath wouldn't freeze their moustaches. But they grafted. No complaints. No panic. Just slow, steady work.

I settled in quickly. Nights suited me. Less noise, fewer people giving orders they didn't understand. Within weeks, I'd earned enough trust that decisions came my way by default. Problems were handed over without argument. It wasn't dramatic. It wasn't loud. Just respect, quietly given.

After a month they pulled me into the office.

"You're stepping up," the superintendent said. "We want you running the whole spread."

Just like that.

From night toolpusher to superintendent.

No politics, no backroom deals, no drama.

It felt good.

More responsibility.

More money.

More proof that I actually knew what I was doing.

They told me the next step was **Turkmenistan**. New drilling programme. Big expectations. They wanted someone reliable — someone who didn't break or moan. The plan was simple: finish Russia, take a short breather, then head out to the desert.

I didn't mind. I'd worked in worse climates. Heat or cold, it was all the same to me as long as the equipment behaved and the men didn't cut corners.

But Russia wasn't without its moments.

One night, halfway through a run, the driller leaned towards me. "Listen," he said. "If the brake fails, you jump. Don't look back. Don't worry about the others. Just jump."

I stared at him. "That bad?"

He shrugged. "Old rig. Russian steel. You know."

I didn't know, but I learned quickly. Every time the brake squealed, my heart hit my ribs like a fist. But the thing held. Somehow. Like everything else out there — rough, ugly, but still hanging on.

Outside of work, life was simple. Eat, sleep, thaw out. The nearest town had a shop where you could buy cigarettes, vodka, and not much else. The women behind the counter watched you like you were about to steal something. The locals didn't speak English, and my Russian didn't go past hello, thanks, and beer. It didn't matter. You didn't come to places like this to socialise.

By the third month, the cold stopped bothering me. The routine settled in.

Work. Sleep. Repeat.

For the first time in years, things felt steady. Predictable.

Too steady, maybe.

Because just when I started thinking ahead to Turkmenistan — thinking about the next step, the next job, the next challenge — life decided to remind me that it didn't care much for my plans.

News was coming.

The kind that didn't wait.

The kind that didn't leave options.

Turkmenistan Prep

Turkmenistan sounded straightforward when they first mentioned it. A desert job. Hot, dry, isolated. After Russia, that didn't bother me. Cold or heat — the work stayed the work. You dealt with whatever the weather threw at you.

The office sent over the briefing pack: maps of **Turkmenistan**, a list of equipment they wanted upgraded, a drilling schedule that looked ambitious for the time frame. None of it surprised me. Companies always planned programmes as if rigs were perfect machines operated by perfect men.

The reality was always a compromise held together by cable ties, swearing, and whoever had the strongest will on shift.

The superintendent pulled me into his office for a proper talk.

"This will be a good move for you," he said. "New field, big potential. You run it well, you're in line for management."

Management.

A word that never meant much to me, but it did mean more responsibility, more control, and more money. And after the shambles in Iran, it felt good to be wanted for the right reasons again.

He walked me through the plan: I'd finish my remaining rotation in **Russia**, then head home for a short break before flying into a staging camp near the Turkmen border. From there, I'd be driven out to the desert to meet the crew and start getting the site ready.

"What's the setup like?" I asked.

He smirked. "Hot. Flat. Nothing for a hundred miles. Bring patience."

I'd worked in places like that.

Heat didn't scare me.

Isolation didn't either.

It was the people you ended up relying on that made or broke a job.

The weeks leading up to departure were a mix of finishing Russian commitments and cramming in everything I needed to know about the Turkmen operation. New contractor. Different supply chain. Their own way of doing things. It was clear early on that they wanted everything done fast but without spending much. A classic combination that never ended well.

Still, the challenge was familiar. And part of me liked that.

You walked into a broken system, figured out what was essential, ignored the rest, and made it work by sheer force of will.

In the camp office, one of the engineers — young lad with glasses steamed from the indoor heating — handed me a stack of reports.

"You'll want these," he said. "Previous campaigns. Problems they never solved."

He wasn't wrong. Most of the reports read the same way:

- poor sand control

- unreliable transport

- morale issues

- supply delays

- heat exhaustion cases every rotation

None of it fazed me. I'd seen worse in places with better marketing campaigns.

My plan was simple: get boots on the ground, see what they had, decide what mattered, and scrap the rest. Ten percent of a job like that was technical. Ninety percent was dealing with people who didn't trust each other.

Before leaving Russia, I phoned home. It had been a while. Calls from remote jobs were either rushed or missed entirely, and my wife had grown used to that rhythm.

"How's everything?" I asked.

There was a pause.

"Fine," she said. But her voice was tight in a way I recognised.

The boys were at school when I called, so I didn't think much more about it. Homesickness comes and goes. You learn not to assume the worst every time someone sounds tired.

Turkmenistan paperwork arrived a few days later — travel documents, medical clearances, emergency contacts. They wanted me on a flight soon after my home break. Everything lined up neatly. Too neatly.

On my last night in Russia, the driller handed me a bottle of vodka.

"For desert courage," he said with a grin.

I laughed and packed it, thinking it'd sit unopened for months. I didn't know that Turkmenistan would never happen. That the next part of my life wasn't going to be heat, sand, or the desert at all.

Something was waiting for me at home. Something that would cut clean through every plan I'd made and send everything sideways in a single moment. And Turkmenistan — like so many things in this line of work — would vanish before it even started.

The Call Home

The flight home from **Russia** felt longer than usual. Maybe it was because I finally had a clear path in front of me — Turkmenistan, a step up, a chance to move into proper management. For once, the next move wasn't chaos. It was planned. Structured. Almost civilised.

I landed, collected my bag, walked through the arrivals gate expecting the usual mix of hugs, complaints about my long absences, and questions about when I'd be off again.

But my wife didn't look relieved to see me.

She looked worried.

"We need to talk," she said as soon as I'd put the suitcase down.

Those are five words you never want to hear when you've just come off a rotation.

We sat at the kitchen table. She took a breath, bracing herself.

"It's our son," she said. "He's been expelled."

I didn't react at first. I just stared at her.

"Expelled? Again?"

She nodded.

"This time it's serious."

She slid a letter across the table. The phrasing was the usual school nonsense — *breach of conduct, inappropriate behaviour, ongoing concerns* — but the meaning was clear. They were done with him.

"What did he actually do?" I asked.

She told me. I won't repeat it here — not because it was unforgivable, but because it was the sort of stupid teenage mess you sort out at home, not something that should derail a kid's life. But the school didn't see it that way, and neither did the others he'd tangled with.

"He's been hanging around with older lads," she added. "Trouble. Drugs."

That word hit me harder than any blowout or near-miss ever had.

"How long has this been going on?"

"A while," she said quietly. "You've been away. I tried to manage it but... he's slipping."

Turkmenistan evaporated right there.

The desert. The promotion. The next step.

Gone in one breath.

I didn't shout. I didn't panic. Offshore life teaches you that panic solves nothing.

I just stood up, grabbed my jacket, and said: "Where is he?"

She told me the estate where he'd been spending time. I knew it. Everyone did. The sort of place where kids drifted toward trouble because there was nothing else to drift toward.

I drove straight there.

He was easy to spot — hood up, hands in pockets, trying to look older than he was. When he saw me get out of the car, his face dropped. Not fear — guilt.

"Get in," I said.

He didn't argue. That alone told me everything.

Back at the house, we sat in the living room. He avoided eye contact, tapping his foot like he was ready to bolt.

"What's going on?" I asked.

He shrugged. "Nothing."

"Don't insult me," I said. "Start talking."

It took time, but it came out eventually — the bad mates, the skipped classes, the weed, the fights, the pressure to act harder than he felt. He wasn't a bad kid. He was lost. Untethered. And I wasn't there to keep him straight.

You can replace a superintendent.

You can't replace a father.

That night, after the house went quiet, my wife said, "Don't go to Turkmenistan. Not now. He needs you."

I already knew that.

The decision had made itself the moment I saw him slouched against that wall.

I emailed the company the next morning.

Family crisis. Will not be travelling.

No timeline for return.

They replied within the hour — polite, disappointed, already moving on.

That's how the industry works.

You're needed until you're not.

The following days were all about fixing what had started to go wrong. Meetings with schools. Phone calls with the council. Clearing out the circle of lads he'd been hanging around with. Laying down rules. Real rules. The kind you enforce, not the kind you hope stick.

He pushed back at first, naturally.

But he came around.

Kids don't hate discipline — they hate absence.

Within a couple of weeks, he straightened up.

Routine. Accountability. A bit of fear. A bit of trust.

The mix worked.

Then came the quiet part — the part every oilman knows too well.

I was out of a job again.

No income.

No next step lined up.

Just responsibility and a bank balance that wouldn't wait forever.

But I didn't regret it. Not once.

Work could wait.

A child couldn't.

And just like that, the Russia–Turkmenistan chapter of my life closed before it truly began.

The next call — the one that would pull me into an entirely different world — hadn't arrived yet.

But it was coming.

Work didn't come straight away. Weeks passed with nothing but bills and the weight of being home without a plan. I'd done the right thing for my son, but the bank didn't care about that, and offshore companies cared even less. A man out of rotation is a man fading from the list.

Then one morning the phone rang — KCA again.

Different tone this time.

A bit of humility.

"We know things ended badly," the man said. "But we need someone. Not Iran. Somewhere else."

I didn't bother pretending I had options.

"Where?"

"Nigeria."

That word sat in the air like a challenge. Dangerous. Chaotic. A place you only sent men when nothing else worked. But I had a family to look after. And poverty has a way of sharpening your decisions. "Fine," I said. "I'll take it." And with that, I stepped into the hardest chapter of my life.

Chapter 12
Into The Delta

Arrival in Nigeria

The heat hit me the second I stepped off the plane in **Port Harcourt** — thick, wet, and close enough to feel like the air was trying to climb inside your lungs. Even the breeze felt heavy. The airport itself was barely controlled chaos: shouting, waving hands, security men with rifles slung low, and queues that moved in every direction except forward.

A man in a faded company shirt stood by the barrier with my name scribbled on a card.

"You Michael?"

I nodded.

"Follow me. No stopping."

He didn't offer small talk. Just turned and pushed through the crowd like he'd learned long ago not to hesitate in places like this. Outside, a wall of taxi drivers surged toward us until two armed escorts stepped in front, using their presence more than their weapons to move people back.

"Welcome to Nigeria," the driver muttered once we reached the vehicle — an armoured SUV with pockmarks in the doors that didn't look decorative.

We drove out through the airport gate at speed. The road wasn't long, but it was enough to get the first sense of the place: half-finished buildings, market stalls, people walking between cars without caring how close tyres came to their toes, and the constant thump of generators behind every wall.

The city didn't feel dangerous in the cinematic sense. It felt unpredictable — like every street had its own rules, and nobody was going to explain them to you.

The compound was a different world entirely. High walls topped with razor wire, armed guards at the gate, and a checkpoint inside the checkpoint. It was built like someone had designed a resort and then remembered halfway through that it needed to survive a minor war.

As soon as we rolled in, the noise changed. The city's hum was replaced by music from the bar, laughter, and the sound of people trying to forget where they were. Men walking around with two or three girlfriends hanging off them. Others drinking like tomorrow wasn't guaranteed — which in this part of the Delta, it wasn't.

The driver looked at me.

"You stay inside after dark," he said. "Simple rule. You break it, we pick you up in a bag."

He said it casually, like it was weather advice.

Inside the accommodation block, the aircon rattled like a dying generator. The room was small but clean, with a bed bolted to the floor and a desk that had seen better decades. There was a laminated card taped to the wall listing evacuation procedures in four languages. The final line read: *If in doubt, lie flat and hope.*

They didn't sugar-coat things here.

That evening I was called to meet the field manager. He was a tall, wiry bloke with the eyes of someone who hadn't slept properly in months. He poured two drinks before speaking.

"You know why you're here?" he asked.

"I assume because someone quit."

He gave a short laugh. "Five. We've had five superintendents in nine months. Contract's on life support. If we lose one more well, the operator pulls the plug and we're done."

I waited.

Men in places like this don't rush the important part.

He leaned forward. "I need someone who won't run, won't panic, and won't bullshit me. They say that's you."

"They say a lot," I answered.

He smiled at that — small, tired, genuine.

"You'll see the rigs tomorrow. They're in the jungle. Proper jungle. Nothing like the desert work you've done."

He took another drink.

"Before we go any further, I need to know something. Out there, there's one rig nobody wants. Worst conditions. Worst crew. Worst maintenance. You want easy, I won't give it to you. But if you want the job that will tell me who you are..."

He let the sentence hang.

I didn't blink.

"Give me the worst rig."

He cracked a grin. "Good. Because that's all we've got left."

He explained the basics: 200 Nigerian workers, one expat — me. Corruption everywhere. Power cuts daily. Roads washed out. Armed escorts mandatory. Two kidnappings in the region this month. Supplies irregular. Morale nonexistent.

"Still want it?" he asked.

"If it drills, I'll run it."

He nodded slowly. "We leave at dawn. Seven-hour drive. Bring water, keep your window closed, and don't get out of the car unless I say so."

Back in my room, I unpacked the bare essentials — boots, gloves, a couple of shirts. The rest stayed in the suitcase. No point making yourself at home in a place that didn't want you to stay very long.

Outside, the compound bar thumped with music. Men danced with their girlfriends like they were on holiday, not hiding behind concrete and razor wire. You could forget where you were if you wanted to. But only until the next morning.

I lay back on the bed, listening to the generator groan through the wall.

Nigeria wasn't welcoming me.

It was sizing me up.

And at first glance, it looked like it expected me to fail just like the others.

Into the Jungle

We left the compound just after sunrise, the air already warm enough that the dust stuck to your skin. Two armed escorts sat in the front of the truck, rifles between their knees, eyes scanning the road even when nothing was there. The manager rode beside me. He didn't speak much. Men who've spent long enough in the Delta save their breath for when things go wrong.

Port Harcourt faded quickly — shops, markets, broken pavements giving way to long stretches of green. Not gentle countryside. This was dense, wet, unforgiving growth. The kind that swallows roads the moment you stop maintaining them. Mud tracks veered off into trees, some wide enough for a vehicle, some barely room for a motorbike. Every now and then we passed a military checkpoint — sandbags, oil drums, a couple of men who looked half-asleep until they weren't.

"This is the easy part," the manager said.

He wasn't joking.

After two hours, the road turned to gravel. After three, the gravel turned to mud. Deep ruts shook the truck hard enough that our teeth clicked. Whenever we slowed, children appeared out of nowhere, waving, smiling, running alongside the tyres like they'd never seen boredom in their lives. Women carried buckets on their heads, moving with a balance you couldn't teach. Men stood in the shade, watching us roll past with expressions that gave nothing away.

The further we went, the more the Delta closed in — vines, trees, water pooled in ditches, insects thick enough to buzz against the windows. Occasionally, we passed a village: corrugated roofs, chickens picking at mud, generators coughing smoke. Life here didn't move fast, but it moved regardless of who was watching.

Seven hours feels like a long time when you're heading deep into a place where nothing looks familiar. Eventually the manager tapped the driver's shoulder.

"Slow down. Nearly there."

At first, all I saw were trees. Then shapes emerged — buildings made from shipping containers stacked like someone had tried to build a fortress from scrap. The camp fence was patched with wire and whatever metal they'd found lying around. Inside, men moved between huts, carrying buckets, tools, tyres. No order. No structure. Just motion.

"This is home," the manager said.

Two hundred Nigerian workers. One expat — me.

As I climbed out of the truck, the heat punched harder than in **Port Harcourt**. Thick, wet, almost physical. Sweat ran down my back before I'd taken three steps. A group of rig hands stopped what they were doing to look at me — assessing, weighing up whether I'd last longer than the others.

One man stepped forward.

"You superintendent?" he asked.

"Yeah," I said.

He nodded once. No welcome. No smile.

"Come. You see rig."

We walked through camp. The ground squelched under boots, a mix of mud and spilled diesel. A line of clothes hung between two containers — shirts, trousers, socks stiff with dust. At the far end, a cooking area smoked with the smell of fish and peppers. No mess hall. No aircon. Just open fires and metal pots.

Halfway across the yard, a man sprinted past chasing a chicken like his life depended on it. Behind him, another shouted something in pidgin that made the rest of the crew laugh. No tension there — just the daily rhythm of a camp running on improvisation.

Then we reached the rig.

Calling it "tired" would've been kind. Rust on rust. Hydraulics patched with tape. Cables hanging like someone had decorated it for a festival. Mud pumps that sounded like they were coughing themselves to death. I'd seen bad rigs before — but this one looked like it needed last rites.

I didn't show a reaction.

If you flinch on day one, you lose the room.

"What about maintenance?" I asked.

The man shrugged. "We try. No parts."

"Supplies?"

Another shrug. "When they come, they come."

The generator choked mid-sentence and belched a cloud of black smoke. A mechanic hit it with a length of pipe. It spluttered back to life, reluctantly.

We walked the deck. Tools were scattered. Lines weren't coiled properly. The driller's cabin had a chair held together with rope. I made mental notes, not comments. You can't fix a place like this with speeches. You fix it with consistency.

Back in camp, the manager introduced me to the "storage area."

It was a container with half the items missing.

"Diesel goes missing," he said. "Anti-venom too."

"Anti-venom?" I asked.

He nodded. "Snakes. Plenty. Big ones. Men get bitten, we treat them if we can. But the medicine... some boys sell it."

Of course they did.

Everything was currency here.

My room was a metal box with a bed, a fan that spun like it was drunk, and walls thin enough to hear every generator cough. Better than nothing. Worse than comfortable.

As evening settled, drums thumped from somewhere outside camp. Voices rose and fell. Dogs barked. The jungle itself hummed — insects, frogs, birds calling in rhythms that didn't match anything I'd heard before.

I stood there listening, letting it all sink in.

Nigeria wasn't loud or chaotic in the way Iran had been.

It was something else — a pressure that built from the moment you arrived, steady and unblinking.

This place didn't just test you.

It watched you.

And it waited to see what you would do next.

Mastery of Chaos

The first week was all observation. You don't storm into a place like this and bark orders unless you're trying to get yourself ignored or worse. I watched the crews, watched how they moved, who they listened to, who they avoided. There were two types of men on that rig: the ones who worked because they were proud of the job, and the ones who worked because they were scared of losing the job. Both groups needed different handling.

The first real problem came three days in. Night shift. Diesel levels didn't add up. You don't lose that much fuel to evaporation unless you're drilling on the surface of the sun. I said nothing at first — just started asking quiet questions. By dawn, I had the picture: a side deal between two pump men and the driver of the nightly supply truck. Diesel was siphoned off, sold down the road, and the books smudged just enough to look believable.

I called the two pump men aside.

"Cut it out," I said. "I know. You know I know. Don't make me choose between firing you and ignoring you."

They looked embarrassed more than scared.

One said, "Super, everybody do it."

"Not while I'm here," I answered. "Do your job. Let me do mine."

They stopped. Not because of fear — but because I didn't shame them. Respect gets paid back twice in places like this.

The next issue was snakes. Not small ones either — thick, dark things that moved under the containers like shadows with muscle. One man got bitten behind the generator shed. They dragged him in, his arm already swelling. When I asked for anti-venom, the medic shrugged.

"Finished, sir."

"Finished or stolen?"

"Stolen."

He said it without shame. Just fact.

We improvised — pressure bandage, cold water, prayer. The man recovered, somehow. After that, I had the medic lock what little stock we had inside my container. If someone wanted anti-venom now, they'd have to go through me.

Then came the fumigation scam.

Every two weeks a man would arrive in a pickup, claiming he was here to "spray for mosquitoes." He'd do a ten-minute walk, wave a hose around, and collect a cash payment from the camp funds — which was a metal box with a padlock anyone could pick with a nail.

I watched him twice. The third time, I took him aside.

"You're doing nothing," I said.

He grinned. "Boss, this Nigeria."

"Fine," I said. "Here's the deal. You still take the money. But half goes to the camp. Food. Soap. Anything they need. Non-negotiable."

He stared at me like nobody had ever suggested fairness before.

Then he nodded. "Okay, boss."

The camp got cleansers and proper washing powder the next week. The men noticed. Word travels fast when money flows differently.

Sundays became beer day. One case for the crew, nothing fancy. The first time I brought it out, the entire yard lit up like someone had installed a stadium floodlight. They drank, laughed, played music on dented speakers. It wasn't much, but it broke the tension that had built under the surface.

The "club incident" happened soon after.

One night the boys dragged me to a shack outside camp — a corrugated hut with a pole in the middle and two women dancing like they were trying to distract the world. It wasn't glamorous. It wasn't even safe. But it was an escape.

I didn't drink much. I kept my eyes open. The place wasn't dangerous in the obvious way — it was dangerous in the way a loose nail is dangerous when you're barefoot. You step wrong once.

I didn't step wrong.

Some of the lads had "local wives" — arrangements that were half companionship, half diplomacy. No judgments. In the Delta, survival takes forms outsiders don't understand. The women cooked, washed clothes, kept order in ways the men couldn't. Everybody got something out of it.

Work improved. Slowly at first, then noticeably. Lines were coiled properly. Tools put back. Pumps repaired instead of slapped with a spanner. The rig didn't look good, but it worked — and in the jungle, function is the only beauty anyone cares about.

The real turning point came when we had to move the rig. Logistics sent us 150 trucks. One hundred and fifty. The driver coordinator nearly fainted. But we moved them. I stood at the front of the convoy, shouting directions, waving my arms until my shoulders went numb. Mud, rain, broken tracks — we kept going. Seven hours, then another seven. The kind of day that breaks men.

At the end, the trucking owner slipped me an envelope. I didn't need to open it to know what it was.

I handed half to the rig boys.

"Share it. All of you."

The reaction was instant. Cheers. Laughter. Trust.

That envelope bought me more than goodwill — it bought authority. Real authority, the kind you can't demand, only earn.

Two days later, the manager called me on the radio.

"You're now supervising more than one rig," he said. "Congratulations. Don't cock it up."

That was Nigeria for you. No certificates. No ceremonies. Just more responsibility when you proved you could take it.

Then came the cesspit incident.

Wolfgang arrived from head office — clipboard in hand, acting like he was the sheriff of the Delta. He strutted around the rig, barking about procedures he didn't understand. Then, walking across the yard, he fell straight into the latrine pit — up to his waist in a slurry nobody should ever swim in.

The crew howled. Someone nearly passed out from laughing. I pulled him out, trying not to gag at the smell.

He looked at me, horrified.

"This is unacceptable!"

I nodded. "You're the one who fell in it, mate."

He left the next day.

Everything seemed to be climbing toward something — progress, stability, control.

But in Nigeria, the climb is always shorter than the fall.

Collapse

The first sign things were turning came with the arrival of the big rig — the **3000-horsepower rig** they'd been talking about for months. It came in pieces on trucks that groaned under the weight, each section wrapped in tarps that flapped like sails. The moment I saw it, I knew the workload was about to triple. Big rigs don't mean big pay. They mean big problems.

Assembly started before dawn most days. Welders shouting, cranes whining, men hauling lines in heat that pressed your spine like a thumb. I spent my time running between crews —

checking lifts, chasing missing parts, straightening out arguments. The pressure never eased. If anything, it grew thicker than the humidity.

Sleep became something I took in slices — twenty minutes here, an hour there, boots still on, radio by my head. Every night shift bled into the next.

Then came the kidnappings.

They didn't touch our camp directly, but they hit another contractor down the road. Men snatched off a pickup at dawn, bundled into the trees, held for ransom. The operator didn't announce it. They never did. But word travels fast when every man knows he might be next. Our escorts doubled. Guns out. Windows up. And every time you heard a truck backfire, half the yard flinched.

By then, I was supervising several rigs, not just one. I'd earned the trust, but trust doesn't protect you from exhaustion. The radio never stopped. Every channel crackled with something urgent — a pump failure, a truck stuck, a driller shouting about pressures. I felt like I was holding seven fires at once, and every one of them wanted to spread.

The malaria hit at the worst possible time.

It started with a headache behind my eyes — a deep, throbbing pulse. At first, I thought it was the heat. Then the shivering came. Not polite shivers either — full-body tremors that made it hard to stand.

I tried to work through it.

Bad mistake.

On the second night, climbing the stairs to the doghouse, my legs went from under me. One moment upright, the next on my knees, gripping the rail like the world had tilted.

A floorhand grabbed my arm.

"Super, you sick."

"I'm fine," I lied.

He shook his head. "You go bed. Now."

I didn't argue. Couldn't, really. Every joint burned. Sweat poured off me even though I was freezing. Back in my container, I curled up under a thin blanket, shaking so hard the metal frame rattled. Someone fetched the medic. He checked my temperature, swore under his breath, and pushed tablets into my hand.

"Malaria," he said. "Lie down. Don't move."

I lay there for two days, drifting in and out — half-dreaming, half-praying. Fever dreams, mostly. Voices. Footsteps outside. Radios squawking. Once, I heard a helicopter and tried to sit up, convinced they were coming for me. They weren't. Nobody was.

By the third day, the fever broke enough that I could stand. I should've stayed put. Instead, I dragged myself back to the rig because everything felt like it depended on me. That's the trouble with being competent — they rely on you even when you shouldn't rely on yourself.

A few shifts later, an injury happened. Minor, and not my fault. A roustabout took a bad step on a slick board and wrenched his ankle. Should've been a formality — incident reported,

186

treatment logged, review done. But head office wanted a name to attach to the paperwork, and mine was the one nearest the top.

The manager called me into the container that served as an office. His face said everything before he opened his mouth.

"They want someone held responsible," he said quietly.

"And?"

He didn't meet my eyes. "They say it's you."

I stared at him. "For a twisted ankle?"

He didn't answer. Couldn't.

It wasn't his decision — it came from people who'd never stepped foot in the Delta. He handed me a paper. "Immediate termination. Pack your things. Escort will take you to the compound."

That was it. No hearing. No argument. No second chance. I walked out into the yard. The men saw my bag and their faces tightened. A few came over.

"Super, you go?"

"Why?"

"What happen?"

I didn't have the energy to explain something that didn't make sense.

"Not your fault," one said. "We know."

I nodded. "Keep the place running."

The ride back through the jungle felt longer than the first time — not because of the distance, but because something in me had cracked. The Delta swirled past the windows: villages, trees, mud, smoke from cooking fires. All the life I'd tried to manage, steer, and survive.

Back at the compound I collapsed onto the bed, fever creeping back, body shaking again. Ten days later, I was on a flight home — thinner, weaker, carrying the weight of a year that felt like ten.

Nigeria hadn't beaten me in skill.

It had beaten me in time, sickness, and unfairness.

And it spat me out the same way it swallows men every day — without ceremony, without thanks, without looking back.

But that wasn't the end.

Not even close.

Chapter 13
The Comeback

Flatlined

Coming home after Nigeria didn't feel like returning. It felt like washing up on a shore you didn't remember leaving. I stepped off the plane grey-faced, sweating through my shirt, legs unsteady. The fever wasn't gone — it had just taken a break to let me get on the flight. By the time I reached the house, I was shaking again, colder than I'd ever been in the Russian winter.

My wife opened the door and stared like she didn't recognise me.

"Jesus, Michael... what have they done to you?"

I tried to speak, but my throat was dry and my head throbbed like someone was driving nails in behind my eyes. I managed, "Bed. Just... bed."

That was where I stayed.

For ten days I barely moved. I drank water when she forced it on me, swallowed tablets without looking at the labels, and drifted in and out of something that wasn't quite sleep or consciousness. Malaria doesn't hit you like a cold; it drags you under, holds you there, and lets you come up for air only when it chooses. Every night, sweat soaked the sheets. Every morning, chills shook the frame of the bed.

At the end of those ten days, I could finally stand without the room tilting. But I'd lost weight, lost strength, lost any sense of direction. Work? Money? Future? All of it felt like some other man's life.

I'd spent almost three decades holding the line — dangerous jobs, dangerous countries, saving other people's messes. And for what? Another company that cut me loose to save face on a report.

One afternoon, sitting at the kitchen table with a blanket around my shoulders, I caught myself whispering a sentence I never thought I'd say out loud:

"I don't know what to do."

That scared me more than anything I'd seen in the jungle.

My wife poured tea and sat opposite. She didn't talk. She didn't tell me to get over it. She just stayed there, letting the silence settle in a way that didn't feel heavy. Eventually she said:

"You've always landed on your feet. You will again."

I wasn't convinced. The bank didn't run on optimism. The bills didn't care that I'd nearly died. And the offshore world moves fast — you disappear for a month, you're yesterday's name.

And I'd been gone much longer than that.

Money slipped through our hands quicker than it came in. I cashed out the last of my Nigeria pay — what was left of it after the "wine, women, and song" chapter everyone goes through eventually — and watched it evaporate on bills, food, and trying to keep everything afloat. Pride doesn't pay electricity. Confidence doesn't pay the mortgage.

One night, lying awake, staring at the ceiling, I whispered something I hadn't said in years:

"Please, God... just give us another oil boom. One more. I'll do the rest."

It wasn't a dramatic prayer. It wasn't spiritual either. It was desperation. Pure and simple. A man talking to the dark because nobody else was listening.

A few days later, my daughter came home from college and found me staring at the laptop like it might bite me.

"Dad," she said, "give me your CV."

"What for?"

"I'm posting it online."

I almost told her not to bother. The industry was flat. Men with better health and cleaner records than mine were struggling. But she'd already taken the laptop from under my hands and typed faster than I could think.

"There," she said. "Done."

She didn't ask for permission. She didn't need it.

Less than twenty-four hours later, the phone started ringing.

At first I ignored it. Unknown numbers. Agencies. Chancers. But on the third call, something made me answer.

A voice said:

"We've seen your CV. Are you available?"

Available.

I almost laughed. I'd never been more available in my life.

"What's the job?" I asked.

"Supervisor position. Dubai. With **Weatherford**."

Dubai.

A real job.

Real money.

A chance to stand upright again.

"When do you need me?"

"Immediately."

I hung up and just sat there, staring at the wall. After everything — the Delta, the sickness, being thrown out without a word — someone finally wanted me again.

Not long after, another call came. This time the voice was different — official, clipped.

"Mr. Reed? This is your union."

I knew that tone.

Something was coming.

"We've reviewed your case with KCA. They owe you compensation."

I blinked. "How much?"

There was a pause.

"A confidential amount. But you will be paid."

I realised then — for the first time in weeks — that my breathing had eased. That the weight pressing on my chest had stepped back a little.

Between the compensation and the Dubai offer, life had shifted — not back to normal, but back within reach. The comeback hadn't started yet. But the ground beneath me had stopped falling.

Dubai and the Turn

The flight to Dubai felt different from every other time I'd travelled for work. Normally you're bracing for the next battle — new country, new problems, new people to manage. This time, I was just grateful to be upright and earning again. My body still ached from the malaria, and my energy wasn't half of what it used to be, but compared to lying in bed shaking for ten days, I felt nearly invincible.

When the plane landed, the heat wrapped around me like a blanket straight out of the oven — dry, heavy, but familiar. I'd forgotten how loud **Dubai** could be. Everything hummed: traffic, aircon, construction, people moving like they'd been wound too tight. Compared to the Delta, it felt like stepping onto another planet.

Weatherford had put me in a serviced apartment. Clean, modern, polished floors you could eat off. After Nigeria, it felt almost dishonest — like I didn't deserve the comfort. I stood under the shower for twenty minutes just letting the water run over me, trying to wash off the last pieces of everything I'd dragged back from the jungle.

The job itself wasn't glamorous. Paperwork. Planning. Supervising smaller operations. But it was steady, the people were competent, and nobody was trying to steal diesel out of the generator or sell anti-venom on the side. You turn up, do the work, go home. For a while, that was all I needed.

Money started building again. Not fast, but steady. Enough to breathe. Enough to sleep without the bank balance flashing behind my eyelids. My strength crept back week by week. I stopped waking in the night expecting gunfire or radios crackling. I even started enjoying the small things — a decent meal, cold aircon, walking into a shop that actually had the items printed on the shelves.

But the union payout was what really changed things.

It came through without warning — a wire transfer so big I stared at the screen for nearly a full minute waiting for the numbers to correct themselves. "Confidential amount" had sounded vague. Vague didn't prepare me for what arrived.

My wife cried when I told her. Not from excitement — from relief.

"You can finally breathe," she said.

Breathing was one thing. Rebuilding was another.

I paid off what we owed. Booked repairs the house needed for years. Put savings aside for the kids. And for the first time in a long time, I felt in control again. Not rich. Not invincible. Just... steady.

A few months into Dubai, I was beginning to think this might be it — a calmer chapter, less danger, less chaos. Maybe the madness had finally run its course.

Then an email arrived.

Short message.

Simple header.

Sender: **Total**.

Michael,

We'd like you back as a company man.

Double your current rate.

Nigeria or offshore — your choice.

Call if interested.

I read it twice.

Then a third time.

Total.

Offering double.

After everything.

I sat there in silence, elbows on the table, hands clasped. Logic said stay in Dubai — safe money, clean job, predictable days. But logic has never driven the oilfield. Experience has. And experience told me something else entirely:

This was the chance to fix what Nigeria had broken.

Going back on my terms — top pay, full authority, no middlemen trying to cover their mistakes by blaming me. Company man isn't a title you take lightly. It's not the same as being a contractor. It's a badge that says: *you're the one they trust to keep the well alive.*

I called my wife. Told her the numbers. Told her the risk. Told her the truth:

"I think I need to take it."

She didn't hesitate.

"Then take it."

I replied to Total that evening. One sentence:

I'm in.

They booked the flights. Offshore posting first. Nigeria after, depending on the well. "You'll be running things properly this time," the coordinator said. "No politics. Just work. We want you because you know what you're doing."

It was the opposite of how KCA had treated me.

And the opposite of how most companies treat men with past conflicts.

Offshore life with Total was clean. Organised. Professional. Everything ran the way drilling should run — decisions based on competence, not panic or fear. I felt like someone had taken all the broken parts of the last few years and lined them up neatly.

Then, two days after I left the platform for a crew change, the well blew.

The news came by radio — a rush of garbled messages, men shouting over static, the kind of noise you know instantly isn't routine.

Nobody died, thank God.

But the rig was badly damaged.

If I'd been there, I would've been the one in the hot seat. The one everyone looked at when things went wrong. The one held responsible.

Walking across the helideck the next morning, I realised something very simple and very clear:

I'd finally stepped back into the right life. Not a clean one. Not a safe one. But the one built for me. And this time, I was climbing for good.

The Climb and the Call

After the blowout, things moved fast. Total kept me on, no hesitation. If anything, the incident proved my worth — not because I'd prevented anything, but because I hadn't been there to take the blame. Offshore work settled into a rhythm: flights, briefings, well plans, long nights staring at gauges and pressures, watching the sea shift under the rig feet like a living thing.

Money was good. Better than anything I'd earned before. I started putting real numbers aside. Not savings — foundations. Paying down the mortgage early. Setting the kids up. Fixing things in the house as soon as they broke instead of waiting six months. That feeling — living without fear — was worth more than the day rate.

But offshore life is addictive in its own way: structured, isolated, predictable. After Nigeria's madness, it felt almost too clean. Too controlled. Like driving on a motorway after years of dirt tracks. I did well, and everyone knew it. Three years passed like that — steady, quiet, profitable.

Then one rotation, something changed.

A recruiter I barely remembered emailed me.

Said he had a friend at **Orix** looking for a man who could take over a tough position.

Short contract. Big money.

Relief man needed urgently.

I wasn't looking to move. But I'd learned something over the years: when a job comes looking for you, there's usually leverage hidden inside it.

So I listened.

The Orix coordinator sounded desperate in that polite, corporate way — asking questions quickly, talking as if decisions had already been made.

"We've had issues with stability. We need someone who won't fold."

That was the kind of line companies used when things were worse than they wanted to admit.

"Fine," I said. "Send the details."

When the contract arrived, I stared at the numbers.

It was more than double what some companies paid for the same work.

Enough to earn in a few months what used to take a year.

I accepted.

The job was meant to be simple: relief rotation for another superintendent. Cover him while he took time off, hand over smoothly, and move on. But on day two, the man quit. Bags packed, helicopter booked, gone before breakfast.

That left me holding everything — logistics, planning, personnel, rig operations, safety audits — the lot.

Orix didn't blink. They wired the bonus immediately and told me to "keep things steady." In oilfield terms, that means "do the job of two men and don't complain."

I didn't complain.

I just worked.

Weeks blurred into months.

Pressure climbed but so did the money.

You start seeing your life in numbers — mortgages disappearing, savings growing, options opening.

For the first time, retirement didn't feel like a fantasy.

Seven houses by the end of it — not because I wanted to brag, but because property was the only safe place to store the chaos-earned cash.

I finished a rotation, flew home, and felt almost proud — a strange emotion after so many years of being blamed for things that weren't my fault.

The next morning, the phone rang.

No greeting. No warm-up.

Just a voice:

"Is that Michael?"

"Yes."

"This is **Exxon**."

If you've spent enough years in the industry, that name hits different. It isn't like getting a call from an agent or a mid-tier operator. Exxon doesn't hire lightly, and they certainly don't cold-call contractors unless they've done their homework.

"We've seen your record," the man said.

"We'd like to discuss a role."

I didn't speak straight away.

Let him fill the silence.

"The rate is"—he paused—"significantly higher than what you're on now."

I almost laughed.

"Higher than Orix?"

"Yes," he said. "Much higher."

For the first time in decades, I had something that felt like real power: choice.

I told him I'd think about it. Not because I needed to — the decision was already made — but because after years of being treated as if I was replaceable, I wanted that moment. That pause where the biggest company on earth waited for my answer.

I hung up and sat on the edge of the bed.

It had taken everything — the warzone in Iran, the corruption in the jungle, the malaria, the sackings, the pay cuts, the nights sleeping in shipping containers — to get here. But I'd got here.

When I called the recruiter back, I kept it simple.

"I'll take it."

Maersk tried to counter with a late offer.

Too late.

Exxon it was.

And that was the moment — quiet, uncelebrated — when the whole arc turned. Not the chaos. Not the danger. Not the politics. Just that one decision. From here on, the climb wasn't luck. It was earned.

Holding the Line

The Exxon contract came through faster than I expected. No back-and-forth, no delays, no excuses. When big companies decide they want you, they don't waste time. They sent the paperwork, flights, and schedule all in one go, as if they'd been preparing it long before they picked up the phone.

I remember sitting at the kitchen table with the contract open, reading it line by line. Not the numbers — I already knew those mattered. It was the wording I cared about. Clear responsibilities. Clear authority. No vague clauses designed to pin blame on the man in the field. Offshore work is dangerous enough without the politics. Exxon knew that. They didn't hide it behind corporate fluff.

My wife looked over my shoulder.

"Is this the one?"

"Yes," I said. "This is the one."

She didn't smile. She didn't need to. We'd been through too much for celebrations. What we felt wasn't excitement — it was stability. And stability had been rare for us.

Before flying out, I took a week to ground myself. Ran errands. Fixed the fence out back. Went for long walks just to enjoy being on actual sidewalks. Ate dinners without a radio crackling in the background. Normal life. I didn't realise how much I'd missed it until I was standing in a supermarket trying to pick a loaf of bread. In Nigeria the "choice" was whatever wasn't mouldy. In Dubai it was whatever cost the least. In England it was rows and rows of it — small reminders of how simple life could be when you weren't running from alarms or dodging trouble.

But normal never lasts in this line of work.

The closer the flight approached, the more I felt that old itch — the one I'd tried to ignore since the jungle. Part nerves, part habit. You don't walk into high-pressure operations without feeling it in your chest. Some men call it fear. Some call it instinct. For me, it's a reminder that I'm stepping into a place where mistakes don't forgive.

The flight was long, the kind that turns hours into something blurry. When I reached the hotel, the coordinator handed me the schedule: safety briefings, induction, chopper to the rig. Straightforward. Clean. Organised. Exactly what you expect from a giant of the industry.

Yet even as I went through the motions, something sat at the back of my mind. A memory, not a warning: standing alone on that Nigerian rig, the only white man in a camp of two hundred, with everyone watching to see whether I'd sink or swim. It was a world away from this new chapter, but it shaped everything. It taught me how quickly things can turn, how little protection there is once the work starts.

The helicopter ride out to the platform was calm — sea like steel, sky clear. I'd sat on a hundred choppers in my life, but this one felt different. Not heavier. Just... earned. It's one thing to be sent to a job because no one else will do it. It's another to be handpicked because they trust you with millions of pounds' worth of equipment and the lives of everyone on site.

When we touched down, I stepped onto the helideck and felt something I hadn't felt in years: authority without the fight. No scrambling for respect, no political battles, no managers trying to cover their incompetence with blame. Just a straight line — do the work, do it well, and everyone wins.

The OIM shook my hand and said,

"Good to finally have you onboard. We've heard a lot."

I didn't ask what exactly they'd heard.

In this business, your reputation travels faster than any aircraft.

The tour of the platform was quick. Everything was in order — systems tight, procedures followed, equipment modern. No rotting cabins, no diesel thieves wandering about after dark, no angry men crowding around the kitchen door demanding wages. After years of chaos, the clean professionalism almost felt unnatural.

But that's the thing about the oilfield: the calmest places often come after the worst storms. And I'd had enough storms to last a lifetime.

That night, I stood outside on one of the walkways watching the flare stack burn against the dark sea. The platform hummed beneath my boots — pumps, generators, the constant heartbeat of offshore life. Somewhere in the distance, lightning flashed behind a wall of cloud, but out here the sky stayed clear.

I thought about all the places that had led me here: Iran, with its empty rig site and bombed-out silence. Russia, cold enough to freeze thought. Turkmenistan, the assignment I never took. Nigeria — chaos, corruption, the jungle swallowing everything and giving nothing back. Dubai, clean and temporary. And now this: a place built on precision instead of luck.

For the first time in decades, I wasn't climbing to escape poverty or fear.

I was climbing because I'd earned the right to choose where I stood.

The next chapter wouldn't be about survival.

It would be about control — financial, professional, personal.

And standing there above the ocean, with the flare lighting the night orange, I understood something simple:

I wasn't running anymore.

I was building.

Chapter 14
The Desert Trap

Work stayed steady after Exxon, steady enough that I started thinking the worst of it was behind me. But the oilfield never stays still. Contracts end, managers move on, money shifts from one corner of the world to another. One month you're flat-out, the next you're staring at a calendar with nothing written on it. When my rotation finished and nothing new came through, I felt that old edge again — the quiet reminder that in this business you're only ever safe while the phone keeps ringing. It didn't take long before it did. A Norwegian outfit, quick start, decent rate. I took it without thinking too hard. Work is work, and gaps are dangerous.

The Norwegian Misfire

The job with the Norwegian outfit came out of nowhere. I'd barely settled after Exxon when the call came: Rig Manager position, good rate, quick start. On paper it looked solid — a chance to run a clean operation without jungle politics or offshore egos. I'd worked for enough nationalities to know every group had its quirks, but Norwegians generally meant structure, procedure, and pay on time. After years of chaos, that sounded almost relaxing.

When I arrived, it was obvious straight off that I was the odd one out.

Only Englishman there.

Everyone else Scottish.

Not a problem in itself — I've worked with Scots my whole career — but this crew had history together, the kind that closes ranks whether you're the enemy or not.

They didn't want a Rig Manager. They wanted their mate in the chair.

The sabotage started on day one. Little things at first: paperwork "misplaced," radios set to the wrong channels, equipment moved without telling me. Petty stuff. But petty becomes dangerous fast on a drilling site. You can't manage a rig if you can't trust the men passing you information.

By the end of week one, it escalated. I'd give an instruction, and someone would quietly undo it behind my back. I'd schedule a safety meeting, and half of them would conveniently vanish. The night pusher wrote reports that made it look like I wasn't even turning up for shifts. They weren't trying to get me fired — they were trying to shove their friend into my seat.

The company, **Noreco**, didn't see it at first. On paper everything seemed fine. Daily reports from the Scots painted a neat little picture of incompetence on my part. They were smart about it — not outright lies, just enough distortion to make it look like I was the problem.

But you can't hide the truth forever.

Not in drilling.

The well tells on you.

They made a mistake one night — forged a set of numbers that didn't match the logs. Management spotted it. They finally dug deeper, interviewed the wrong man first, and the whole story came out like pus from a boil.

The company called me in.

"Michael, it appears there's been... misrepresentation."

I just stared at them. "Is that your word for it?"

They apologised.

Privately, quietly, the way companies do when they're embarrassed.

Told me I'd done everything right. Told me the crew had undermined the operation. Told me action would be taken.

But none of that mattered.

The project was collapsing anyway.

Funding issues.

Logistics issues.

Management arguing with itself.

The whole thing was already sinking before I'd ever walked through the gate.

Two days later, they shut the job down entirely.

And then something strange happened.

Payroll called me in and handed over a figure: **£40,000**.

For one month.

"Compensation," they said. "For the stress and the disruption."

I'd been in the industry twenty-eight years and never once heard a company pay a man for "stress." Most men are lucky if they get an apology. I took the money, shook their hands, and walked out with the same thought in my head:

I didn't win. They just paid me to leave the mess behind.

When I got home, my wife looked at me the way she always did after I returned from another failed circus — half relieved, half waiting to hear what had gone wrong this time.

"Over already?" she asked.

"Over," I said. "They paid me to disappear."

She gave a short laugh. "Only you could get sacked with a bonus."

I didn't correct her.

It wasn't worth explaining.

The truth was simple: the job had died before I ever stepped onto it. I'd just been the outsider who walked into a family argument and took the punch meant for someone else.

But underneath the frustration, something else was brewing — a feeling I'd had before, one I recognised instantly.

The itch for the next job.

At this point in my life, the gaps between contracts felt dangerous. Too much time at home meant too much thinking, too much remembering. I needed work. Structure. A direction.

And the industry was shifting again — whispers of new contracts, new operators, new money. Rumours about the Gulf heating up. That was enough to keep me looking.

It didn't take long.

A message came from a coordinator at **Kuwait Oil Company**.

They were staffing up.

Big project.

Long-term roles.

Then one sentence that stuck out like a beacon:

"We need experienced men. Proper ones."

I replied within the hour.

Within a week, I was packing again.

The Norwegian disaster faded behind me as fast as it had arrived. What waited ahead was Kuwait, the buffer zone, the politics, the danger — and one of the biggest climbs of my career.

But I didn't know any of that yet.

All I knew was this: I had one foot back in the game.

The Grey Wolf Turnaround

Kuwait felt like stepping into a different kind of heat — not the punishing, airless wall from Nigeria, but a dry furnace that sat in your lungs and made every breath feel like you were sucking air out of an oven. Still, it was organised. Structured. Nothing like the jungle or the desert chaos I'd crawled through before.

The job was with **Kuwait Oil Company**, but they placed me on a **Grey Wolf Drilling** rig. Big contract. High expectations. And a history of underperformance that everyone pretended wasn't their fault.

The Americans had taken twelve months to drill a 20,000-foot well. A full year. KOC wasn't happy, and they didn't hide it. Their tone at the induction was simple enough: *fix it or leave.*

When I reached the rig, it was obvious why the previous team had struggled. Everything looked technically correct, but the atmosphere was wrong. Too many men standing around waiting for someone else to decide things. Decision-making spread thin across layers of people who were terrified of upsetting the next man up the ladder. It wasn't incompetence — it was hesitation. And hesitation kills wells.

I spent the first few days watching. Not interfering. Just watching. Looking for the gaps. You can tell a lot about a rig by its silences — the pauses between instructions, the delays between a command and its execution. On this one, every silence was half a second too long.

So I made changes.

Not dramatic ones. Just the stuff that needed doing.

Tightened the chain of command.

Cut the pointless paperwork.

Shifted responsibilities to the men who actually knew what they were doing instead of the ones with the loudest opinions.

Created a rhythm the well could follow.

Within a week the rig felt different. You can sense momentum long before you see it on the charts. Connections were cleaner. Pipe movement smoother. Fewer questions being lobbed up the chain because people already knew the answer.

KOC noticed.

Grey Wolf noticed.

Everyone noticed.

The well we were drilling – same formation, same depth target – was finished in three months. Not twelve. Three. Even I had to step back and blink at that. But success in drilling is never one man's glory. It's the team coming together and finally trusting the process instead of the politics.

My back-to-back took over next rotation and kept the pace. Another three months, another clean finish. No excuses. No breakdowns disguised as "operational delays."

The whispers started after that.

"How are they doing it?"

"Why couldn't the Americans manage this?"

"Who's running that rig?"

People like to pretend performance is about equipment or budgets. It isn't. It's about leadership — the right man in the chair, the rest of them knowing someone has the wheel.

Then came the delegation visit.

A small convoy of white SUVs rolled into the desert like they were arriving at a royal inspection. KOC men in pressed white dishdashas, sunglasses permanently in place, faces giving nothing away. They toured the site with slow, measured steps, taking notes without saying a word.

We finished another well shortly after they left. Fast. Clean. Record time for the field.

A week later, I got the call.

"Michael, you're being promoted."

Just like that. No warm-up.

"You'll be Senior Company Man over three rigs — Grey Wolf, **Nabors**, and **Weatherford**."

Three rigs.

Three entirely different crews.

Three entirely different sets of problems.

I should have felt proud. And part of me did. But the other part knew exactly what was coming: pressure, politics, and an even bigger target on my back. The crews were mostly Asian and Russian. Hard-working, capable, but handled badly by previous managers. They'd been spoken down to for years by people who had no idea what they were doing. On the first day of my new posting, I watched two company men argue over a pressure reading they didn't understand. Not incompetence — arrogance disguised as authority.

I fired them both.

Not with shouting. Just a sentence:

"You're done. Transport will take you back."

Word spread fast after that.

Some respected it.

Some hated it.

The ones who hated it weren't shy about showing it.

But I've learned something in my career: if they don't respect your competence, make them respect your consequences. The work picked up pace. Wells drilled efficiently across all three rigs. Numbers improved. KOC held meetings where my name kept appearing at the top of their performance charts. But success doesn't stop resentment — it sharpens it. Some men don't want to rise with you; they want to see you fall.

That tension built every week. Quiet glances. Mutters in languages I couldn't understand but didn't need to. A feeling I'd had before — that someone was waiting for the right moment to stick a knife in.

They found their moment soon enough.

And it didn't come from work. It came from a place no one expects trouble: a hospital. Where I met her.

The Nurse and the Trap

The hospital in Kuwait was the cleanest building for fifty miles in any direction. White tiles, cold aircon, and staff who moved like they were permanently half an hour behind schedule. I went in for something minor — a check-up, a bit of pain across the ribs I'd carried since Nigeria — nothing dramatic. That's where I met her.

She couldn't have been more than mid-twenties. Chinese. Soft-spoken. Efficient. The kind of calm you don't see often in that part of the world. Most of the staff were overworked and underpaid, but she still moved with that careful precision you only find in people who haven't been ground down yet.

Her English wasn't perfect, but it was enough.

"You work on the rig?" she asked.

"Yes."

"You work too much," she said, tapping the chart.

I laughed. "Everyone here does."

We talked while she checked my vitals. Small things. Where she came from. How long she'd been in Kuwait. Whether she had anyone looking out for her. She didn't. Most of the medical staff lived in dorm-style housing, cramped and miserable, stuffed with workers from all over Asia who were there on short-term visas with no rights. She was earning pennies. No one cared.

When I left, she said, "If you need help again, you come back."

I didn't think much of it. But she stayed in my mind.

A week later I asked my driver to take me by the hospital again. I found her outside, waiting for a shuttle. She smiled, surprised.

"You came back," she said.

We spoke properly that time. She told me about the conditions she lived in. The tiny room. The deductions the agency made for everything — food, transport, electricity. She was sending most of her pay back home. I've seen rough conditions in my life, but that was a different kind of rough: invisible suffering, the stuff nobody writes reports about.

I made a decision then.

A small one, or so I thought.

"Every week," I told the driver, "pick her up. Bring her to the rig for a rest day. I'll pay you for the travel."

It wasn't a romance — not at the start. It was two people who saw something familiar in each other: exhaustion, and a life built around everyone else's needs.

But out there in the desert, isolated from everything, things happen faster. She started spending the night when she visited, sleeping in my room, quiet as a ghost. She didn't ask for anything. She didn't take anything. She just wanted peace. And I didn't mind the company.

The problem wasn't her.

It was the men I'd fired.

The Pakistani and Indian company men who'd lost their posts because they were incompetent didn't forget the humiliation. They watched me. Every move. Waiting for anything

216

they could twist into a weapon. They saw the driver picking her up. They saw her walking to my cabin. They didn't know who she was, so they assumed what suited them best: prostitute.

And once they had that story, they didn't wait.

One evening there was a knock at my door.

Hard. Urgent.

I opened it to find five men from the office — not workers, not supervisors, but management. You can always tell the difference from their shoes. They pushed past me without asking.

"Where is she?" one of them demanded.

"Who?"

"The woman. The prostitute."

I laughed at first, thinking it was some kind of sick joke. But their faces were stone.

"She is here illegally," another said. "This is a Muslim country. Do you understand what will happen to her?"

They didn't wait for my answer.

"She can be stoned," he said. "Buried to the neck. Tribal law. It still happens."

Then the next part, aimed straight at me:

"And you will go to military prison."

The room felt smaller instantly. Not because of fear — fear comes later — but because of the sheer stupidity of what they were saying. They didn't care who she really was. They didn't care what the truth was. They just wanted blood, and I was the easiest man to spill it from.

"I need ten minutes," I said. "Let me talk to her."

They hesitated. Authority only carries weight when the man in front of you uses it with confidence. I kept my voice steady. After a moment, they nodded.

I walked into the small back room where she kept her bag. She looked up, confused, half-dressed, hair tied back loosely.

"You need to go," I said quietly.

She didn't ask questions. That told me everything about the kind of life she'd lived.

I opened the rear door and looked across the sand. My driver was there, waiting by the vehicle — headlights off, engine idling. He saw my face and didn't hesitate.

"Take her," I told him. "Don't stop."

She climbed in.

He sped off into the dark, tyres spinning up dust.

I shut the door and walked back inside.

"She's gone," I said.

They didn't believe me.

And the calm before the real trouble began didn't last long.

The Run

They tore the room apart after she left. Opened cupboards, checked under the bed, even lifted the mattress like she might be flattened underneath it. Five grown men scrambling around in pressed office shirts, sweating through their collars, desperate to catch a woman who was already miles away. If it hadn't been so serious, it would've been funny.

"She is here," one of them insisted.

"No," I said. "She's not."

They didn't like that answer.

But they couldn't find her, and that frustrated them even more. When people in power can't locate the person they want to punish, they turn on the next target in reach.

Me.

One of them pointed a finger in my face.

"You have disgraced this company."

I almost laughed. Not because it was amusing, but because of the absurdity. I'd turned their drilling performance around, kept three rigs on track, fired the dead weight they refused to deal with, and somehow the crime that mattered most was offering a nurse a day's rest.

But this wasn't about company policy.

It was about appearance.

About men terrified of losing face in front of other men.

"We will take you to the authorities," he said.

"In the morning," another added. "They only process foreign offenders during daylight."

That last sentence landed differently. Not a threat — a schedule.

Daylight.

I had until then.

As soon as they left, I sat on the edge of the bed and let the room go quiet. I've been in danger before. Real danger. You get to know the texture of it — the way the body goes calm instead of panicked, the way thoughts line up neatly because there's no space for anything else. This wasn't the jungle or the Niger Delta, but the stakes were high all the same. Military prison in **Kuwait** isn't a place you walk out of quickly.

I needed a way out, and I needed it now.

I called the "top man in town" — the office lead, the one with actual authority. Explained the situation, the lies, the set-up.

His response:

"Michael... I cannot interfere. You must deal with it yourself."

Useless.

Cowardly, but predictable.

Fine. That left one option: disappear before dawn.

I threw everything I owned into a bag. No folding, no organising. Essential paperwork. Passport. Cash. Phone charger. The rest could rot in the desert for all I cared.

Outside, the night was black and wide, the rig lights throwing long shadows across the sand. The air tasted of dust and diesel. I walked straight to the transport truck — the one that ran supplies back to the city. The driver was half-asleep, slouched over the wheel.

"You're taking me out," I said.

He blinked at me. "Now?"

"Now."

He didn't ask questions. Smart man. Men who survive in these places know when to shut their mouth and drive.

We pulled out of the compound and headed towards the buffer zone — ten miles of nothingness leftover from the Gulf War. A place no one lingered. A place where mistakes vanished forever.

The road wasn't really a road. More like a strip of flattened sand with tyre tracks deep enough to swallow a boot. Every mile took concentration. The driver kept glancing at me, as if checking whether I was sure.

I was sure.

Halfway through, we saw them — the militia. Not soldiers. Not UN. Just armed men in mismatched uniforms, standing around a burnt-out hut like it was a checkpoint. They didn't wave us down, but they watched the truck crawl past, eyes sharp, rifles resting against their chests.

If they'd decided to stop us, that would've been it.

No paperwork.

No questions.

Just two men in the wrong place at the wrong time.

But they let us go.

The city lights appeared eventually, faint at first, then spreading out like a low fire on the horizon. I told the driver to take me straight to **Kuwait International Airport**. I walked into the terminal looking like any other exhausted contractor heading home. Nobody stopped me. Nobody asked why I was flying at one in the morning. Contractors come and go at all hours; that's the one advantage of this life.

At the check-in desk, the woman looked at my passport, tapped a few keys, and said, "Next flight is 01:30. Amsterdam."

"Book it," I said.

"Reason for travel?"

"My dad had a stroke."

The lie came out clean, easy. Years of dealing with managers and governments teaches you how to lie without blinking.

I boarded the plane twenty minutes later. When the wheels lifted off the runway, I felt the first breath of safety. Not comfort — that comes later. Just safety. A thin blanket separating me from the men who wanted to bury someone to the neck to make a point.

We landed in Amsterdam at dawn. While I was still waiting for my bag, my phone rang.

A Kuwaiti number.

The office.

"Michael," the voice said, "you must report to the office immediately. You are in serious trouble."

I looked out at the grey European sky, breathed in the cold air, and said:

"Fuck you. I'm somewhere you can't get me."

Then I hung up.

That was Kuwait finished.

And a new chapter waiting to start.

Chapter 15
The Last Port

By the time I left Kuwait, I knew the road behind me was longer than the one ahead. I'd pushed as far and as hard as a man could in the oil game, and I'd come out the other side still standing—barely, but standing all the same. What lay next wasn't another country or another rig. It was something else entirely. Before I could step into it, I found myself looking back at the people who'd shoved me forward in the first place, the ones who'd shaped the way I worked and the way I lived. You don't think about that when you're fighting fires every day. But when the dust settles, you see the tracks more clearly.

The Men Who Set Me on My Way

I can trace most of my life back to a handful of people, and none of them would ever call themselves mentors. They were just men who said something at the right moment, or pushed me in a direction I didn't know I needed. At the time, you don't think much of it. You're too busy trying to make enough money to stay out of trouble. But later, with a bit of distance, you realise the weight of it.

The first was **Frank Smeeton**, the bloke who changed my entire future in a single conversation, though neither of us knew it then. I was sat in the pub, same as always, half-bored and half-worried about where my life was heading. Frank came in, pint in each hand, and dropped himself on the stool next to me. He'd heard I was good with tools and didn't mind graft. "Get yourself to Aberdeen," he said. "They're crying out for men on the rigs. Money's good. Work's rough. Perfect for you."

That was it. No speech. No fatherly guidance. Just a straight line from a man who didn't sugar-coat anything. I listened because he didn't dress it up. I've never liked fancy talk. I booked a train the next day, and within weeks I was on my way to the North Sea. Frank never asked for thanks, and I doubt he even thought about it again. But that push set everything in motion: the danger, the money, the travel, the mistakes, the victories, all of it.

Another was **Terry Tucker** from Total. I met him years later, long after I'd picked up enough scars to know what the industry was really like. Terry was sharp—quiet, but sharp. He had the eyes of someone who'd seen every type of bloke come and go. He didn't talk rubbish, and he didn't pretend the job was anything but hard. He told me straight that Total needed a company man, someone who actually knew what they were doing, not someone who only knew how to talk. He didn't butter me up. He just laid it out: "You'd be good at it, Mike. Give it a go."

I'm not easily convinced, but when a man like that says you've got something, you listen. That offer changed the trajectory of my life again, and put real money behind the work. I was ready for it by then. The years in Nigeria, Iran, and all the rest had built something in me—competence, confidence, even if I didn't call it that at the time. Terry saw it before I did.

Then there was my dad. He never taught me a trade, or showed me how to be a man. What he taught me was money. Or rather, the lack of it. My dad had a simple approach: if you wanted something, you earned it. He never bailed me out. He didn't believe in cash gifts or handouts. At the time I thought it was harsh. But when you hit adulthood and realise no one is coming to save you, you understand the value of it. I think that lesson saved my life more than once. I refused to end up skint, relying on someone else's goodwill. That fear—poverty, uselessness—drove me harder than ambition ever could.

There were others who shaped me without meaning to. The Americans in Kuwait—the tool pushers and drillers who could run a team like a machine. They didn't shout unless they had to. They didn't play politics. They just worked, did the job right, and looked after their crews. Watching them in action reminded me what proper leadership looked like. No big speeches. No chasing status. Just doing the work cleanly and straight.

All of these men, in different ways, knocked something solid into me. Determination, mostly. A kind that didn't come from self-help books or motivational posters. It came from stubbornness and pride and a refusal to quit. In Devon we've got a saying: *Devonshire born and bred, strong in the arm and thick in the head.* I've always liked that. There's truth in it. Not the thick bit—well, maybe sometimes—but the strength. Not just physical, but the kind that keeps you on your feet when everything around you is trying to knock you down.

If I've had any success in my life, it's because I kept going. Not gracefully. Not wisely. Just relentlessly. And I wouldn't have

226

managed that without those early nudges from men who probably didn't realise how much they were giving me. They didn't show me how to live, but they showed me where to start. The rest I figured out the hard way.

Exxon, Nigeria, and the End of the Oilfield Road

When the Kuwait job ended, I thought I'd roll straight into the next one, same as always. That's how the oil game works when you've got a reputation: one rig shuts down, another opens up, and you just keep moving. But for the first time in years, there was nothing. No calls, no whispers, not even a rumour. The industry had gone quiet, and quiet is dangerous. Quiet means boredom, and boredom means bills. After a few weeks of pretending it didn't bother me, I accepted the truth: I was out of work.

I called **Techniques**, the agency I'd used on and off over the years. They'd always been straight with me. If they had something, they'd tell me. If they didn't, they wouldn't waste my time. Tommy answered—same voice, same dry tone as ever. "You picked a good time to call, Mike. ExxonMobil are desperate for men in Nigeria. Experienced ones. Not the paper-pushers."

I'd been to Nigeria enough times to know the score. Corruption, heat, danger, long hours. But it didn't matter. When the money's right and the cupboards are looking thin, you don't get picky. I told him I'd take it before he'd even finished explaining the contract.

Within two weeks, I was on a plane again. No excitement, no nerves—just the old familiar feeling of heading back into the grind. Port Harcourt hadn't changed. The airport smelled the same: heat, sweat, diesel. The guards were the same mix of bored and twitchy. The drive through the city still felt like threading a needle through chaos.

Exxon had me supervising a workover rig—nothing glamorous, but steady. The camp was rough, but after the places I'd lived in Iran and the jungle setups I'd survived, it barely registered. I'd worked in worse. I'd slept in worse. The job itself was straightforward: keep things moving, keep the crew safe, keep the well under control. The younger lads looked at me like I'd crawled out of a history book. Most hadn't worked with someone who'd done the full circuit—North Sea, Middle East, Africa, Russia, the lot. They didn't say much, but you could see it in the way they watched.

It was meant to be a short contract. Three months, maybe six. But the job kept stretching, and I kept signing the extensions. One month became three. Three became six. Before I knew it, I'd done a year, then more. The place had a way of swallowing time. The money was good, and the rhythm of the work was familiar. I didn't have to think too hard, and at my age, that's a blessing.

Then **COVID hit**, and everything stopped. We'd heard the early stories, same as everyone else, but no one on the rigs took it seriously at first. You live in close quarters your whole life; you see more illnesses in a month than most people do in a year. But this one was different. The companies panicked before the workers did. Exxon shut down the operation almost overnight. One meeting, one memo, and that was it: all expats terminated, effective immediately. No arguments, no negotiations. Pack your bags, flights arranged, thanks for your service.

Just like that, the job was gone. Not paused—*gone*. We all knew what that meant. When big companies pull the plug during a global crisis, they don't plug it back in when things calm down. They cut deep and they cut fast.

I flew back to England unsure of what came next. For the first time in decades, I started thinking seriously about whether my time in the oilfields was coming to an end. I told my wife I might have to head back to the Middle East. It was the only region still in motion, even with the pandemic ripping through the world. She didn't argue, but she didn't like it.

A few days later, I sat down with my accounts. Proper look, not just a glance. I added everything up: investments, savings, pensions, houses. Eight houses, to be exact. Then I looked at the numbers again because I thought I'd made a mistake. **£2,000,000**, all in. Real money, not the kind that disappears on tax or fees. I sat there for a long time, just staring. The room felt quiet in a way I wasn't used to. Not the quiet of being out of work—the quiet of realisation.

For forty years I'd been chasing money without ever stopping long enough to see how much I'd caught. Fifteen countries, God knows how many rigs, enough bad meals and dangerous shifts to fill five books... and I'd come out of it with enough to never lift another spanner if I didn't want to.

I was sixty-one. Not young, not old, but old enough to feel the miles in my bones. And suddenly the choice was mine for the first time in my life. No agent pushing, no bills forcing my hand, no manager screaming for a replacement. Just me, the bank balance, and the question I'd never been brave enough to ask: *Had I finally earned the right to stop?*

It didn't feel like victory. It felt strange, unsteady, like stepping off a moving train. But it was real. I'd done my part. I'd gone further than I ever expected, and somehow—against every odd—I'd ended up with enough.

Enough to rest.

Enough to breathe.

Enough to start thinking about a life that wasn't measured in wells drilled.

And with that, the oilfield chapter of my life finally began to close. Not with a blowout, not with a firing, not with some grand moment. Just a quiet end, the kind that sneaks up on you when you're not looking.

Life After the Rigs

Stopping work wasn't the hard part. Staying stopped was. When you've spent forty years living out of bags, flying in and out of countries, managing crews, fixing problems, and keeping men alive in the middle of nowhere, normal life feels too quiet. Too still. I tried to treat it like a holiday at first, but after a few weeks of sitting around, I realised something: I had no idea how to be retired. I'd gone from running entire drilling operations to standing in my own kitchen wondering what to do with the day.

So I took the first job that came to me—a hearse driver. It wasn't a career move. It wasn't anything, really. It was just something to get me out of the house. Death has never bothered me; after everything I'd seen offshore and in the deserts and jungles, a silent passenger in the back of a car didn't raise my pulse. The work was simple: pick up, drop off, keep the uniform clean. I did eighteen months of that, cruising around the south coast, carrying men and women who didn't need conversation or supervision. It was a strange sort of peace, and for a while it suited me fine.

But England has a way of closing in on you. The weather, mostly. Grey skies that sit on your shoulders like a damp coat. After years of heat and dust, the drizzle felt like a punishment. My wife felt it too. We'd always talked about spending more time in Spain—we'd bought a place there years earlier when the money was flowing—and one day we just decided to go. No big plan. No deadline. We packed what we needed, locked up the house, and flew south.

Spain was everything England wasn't: warm, open, laid-back. Nothing rushed. Nothing frantic. I felt lighter within a week. I bought a Harley Davidson; always wanted one but never had the time to justify it. Out there it made sense. Long, open roads, good weather, and bikers everywhere. I fell in with a few local clubs—not gangs, just blokes who liked riding—and most days we'd end up criss-crossing the hills or heading down the coast for a drink. No pressure. No politics. For the first time in years, I wasn't responsible for anyone's safety.

The trouble with peace is that it can get dull once you've had too much of it. I needed a purpose, something small, nothing like the rigs. Just a job to keep the brain ticking. So I started doing taxi runs for holidaymakers—airport runs, mostly. Simple work. Good money in cash. You pick up a family, load their bags, get them to the airport, and they treat you like you've solved their problems for them. It made me laugh sometimes. After dealing with blowouts and H_2S alarms and men losing fingers, carrying suitcases felt like a luxury.

One night I got chatting with a bloke who ran a handful of brothels in the area. Not the seedy, backstreet sort—proper licensed places, clean and regulated, the kind that have been part of Spain's economy longer than most people realise. He was short of drivers for the girls, getting them to and from work safely. I wasn't shocked. After Nigeria and Iran, nothing shocks you. So I took the job. Nights, mostly. Pick them up, drop them off, keep an eye out. They were good company—sharp, funny, streetwise. They didn't pretend to be anything they weren't, and I respected that.

That little sideline grew legs. Word spread that I was reliable, discreet, and didn't ask stupid questions. Before long I was doing airport runs in the day, brothel runs at night, and hiring a couple of drivers to take the overflow. Then three drivers. Then five. Nothing official. No brand name. Just a network of people who knew I'd sort them out if they needed a lift, no matter the hour. It wasn't oil money, not even close, but I didn't need oil money anymore. This was pocket money—fuel for the Harleys, nights out, odd jobs around the house.

Life in Spain settled into a rhythm. Early mornings with coffee on the terrace. Rides along the coast. Picking up passengers. Meeting all sorts—retirees, tourists, workers, girls from the clubs, lads looking for a night out. It reminded me that the world is full of people just trying to get by. Not heroes. Not villains. Just people with their own battles.

I didn't miss the rigs as much as I thought I would. What I missed was the clarity of the work—the straight lines, the problems you could see and fix with your hands. But the blood and adrenaline? I'd had enough of that to last ten lifetimes. The older I got, the more I realised that survival isn't just about getting through the danger. It's about knowing when to step away from it.

Spain wasn't an ending. It was a shift. A new kind of graft. A slower life with its own strange edges. And after everything I'd put myself through—from the North Sea to the deserts to the jungles—it felt earned. Not given. Earned the long way.

What It All Added Up To

Looking back over forty years, I don't see a grand plan or a clear path. I see a string of decisions made because there was a bill due, or a chance to earn more, or a job no one else wanted. I see flights I barely remember, camps that felt temporary even after months, men I worked with for a single hitch who still sit in my mind because of one moment—good or bad. I see mistakes, a few victories, and a lot of graft. Mostly graft.

People talk about careers like they're built with purpose. Mine wasn't. Mine was built on not stopping. Every time something knocked me sideways, I got back up and looked for the next job. Not because I was brave, but because I was scared of standing still. Fear has shaped my life more than ambition ever did. Fear of being broke. Fear of being useless. Fear of letting down the people who depended on me. Funny how fear can push you further than confidence.

If there's a thread running through my life, it's that I kept walking into situations that didn't make sense on paper— dangerous places, broken rigs, crooked managers, jobs with no guarantee of safety or sanity. But those were the jobs that paid, and those were the jobs I was good at. Anyone can work when everything's tidy and controlled. I made my living in places where nothing made sense until you forced it to.

What surprises me most now, sitting in Spain with no alarms going off and no radios crackling in the background, is how calm it feels. For decades, life was a constant state of readiness. Even when you slept, part of your brain stayed alert. A noise outside the cabin. A shout in the corridor. A rumble in the pipes. You learned to wake instantly, before your eyes opened. It's a skill, but one that takes a piece out of you every time.

Now the only thing that wakes me up is the sun coming through the curtains or my phone buzzing with a passenger wanting a lift. And instead of leaping out of bed, I just lie there for a moment, enjoying the fact that no one's in danger and nothing needs fixing. It took me years to get comfortable with that. Still not sure I'm fully there.

A lot of people assume the money was the best part of my career, but they're wrong. The money mattered—of course it did—but it wasn't the real payoff. The real payoff was self-respect. Knowing I'd dragged myself out of the kind of life that eats men whole. Knowing I hadn't quit when I was sick, or scared, or exhausted, or at the mercy of someone who wanted me gone. The oilfield doesn't hand out medals, but it shows you who you are. And I learned I could take a hit and keep moving. That's worth more than any paycheque.

My family paid a price for my choices. I missed birthdays, school events, anniversaries. I missed normal life. That's the truth of it. Anyone who says you can have it all is lying. The rigs take their cut in time, and time is the one thing you can't earn back. But I did what I thought was right: I provided. I kept the roof solid and the cupboards full. I gave my kids a better start than I had. It wasn't perfect, but it was honest.

Now the pressure is gone. No one's timing me. No one's demanding paperwork or shouting down the radio or sending me to another country because someone else messed up. I'm not climbing anything anymore. Not ladders, not ranks. I'm just living. I didn't expect to end up escorting girls to work and driving tourists to the airport, but it suits me. It's work without politics. People are grateful for the help, and they pay on time. After what I've been through, that's luxury.

Sometimes, while I'm riding the Harley along the coast or waiting at the airport for a flight to land, I catch myself thinking how strange it all is. From blowouts to brothels. From gas alarms to pensioners with oversized suitcases. From the North Sea to the Spanish sun. If someone had told the nineteen-year-old version of me where I'd end up, he'd have laughed. Or assumed I'd failed somewhere along the way.

But that's the thing: this isn't failure. This is what it looks like when a man survives the long haul. When he does the hard jobs, takes the hits, stays standing, and comes out the other side with his bank balance intact and his life still his own. You don't notice the change while it's happening. You only see it when the noise stops.

If there's a lesson in any of this—not for readers, but for myself—it's that I went further than I ever meant to. I didn't plan a career. I lived one. And at the end of it, when I finally had the chance to stop, I realised I'd earned the right to sit still for a while.

Not because I was clever.

Not because I was lucky.

Because I kept going.

That's all.

In the end, it wasn't the money, or the titles, or the places stamped in my passport that mattered. It was that I'd started with nothing and finished on my own terms, still standing, still myself. I didn't climb by being clever or lucky—I just kept turning up. And if that's the only thing people remember about me, it's enough.

****

www.ingramcontent.com/pod-product-compliance
Lightning Source LLC
Chambersburg PA
CBHW070912130626
46555CB00001B/99